Right to DREAM

38

UNIONTOWN PUBLIC LIBRARY

MEMORIAL BOOK

Right to DREAM

Immigration Reform
and America's Future

WILLIAM A. SCHWAB

The University of Arkansas Press
Fayetteville
2013

Cover photos: Top left and right: Luis Aguilar (left) and Rosa Velazquez (right) hold signs at a DREAM Act rally held in Fayetteville, Arkansas on May 17, 2012. The rally was organized by the Arkansas Coalition for DREAM, a United We DREAM affiliate and, along with other rallies held nationwide, directly contributed to President Obama's announcement on Deferred Action for Childhood Arrivals in June 2012. Bottom photo: Luis Martinez and Claudia Chavez of the Arkansas United Community Coalition at a rally calling for the cessation of mass deportation and separation of immigrant families. The rally was one of the events organized for a conference hosted by the Southeast Immigrant Rights Network in Raleigh, North Carolina on July 13, 2012. Photos by Mireya Reith. All photos provided courtesy of Arkansas United Community Coalition.

Copyright © 2013 by The University of Arkansas Press

ISBN-10: 1-55728-638-8
ISBN-13: 978-1-55728-638-3
e-ISBN: 978-1-61075-526-9

17   16   15   14   13   5   4   3   2   1

♾ The paper used in this publication meets the minimum requirements of the American National Standard for Permanence of Paper for Printed Library Materials Z39.48–1984.

Library of Congress Control Number: 2013930787

For America's 2.1 million undocumented youth,
who dare to dream

CONTENTS

FOREWORD

So, you have decided to learn more about the DREAM Act. I cannot encourage you enough. The path that led me to support the DREAM Act began in May 2008 when the Arkansas Department of Higher Education advised Arkansas universities that offering in-state tuition to students who did not possess a social security number might violate federal law. Up to that point, if undocumented students graduated from an Arkansas high school and satisfied other academic requirements, they were permitted to enter the university and pay in-state tuition. Now, qualified students who grew up in Arkansas would be forced to pay almost $9,000 more a year in out-of-state tuition.

Investigation determined that the University of Arkansas, where I became chancellor in July 2008, had nineteen such undocumented students on campus. All of these students were faced with dropping out, effectively priced out of a college education. By supporting these undocumented students, however, we risked immediately alienating a vocal segment of university stakeholders who felt these students had no place in the university. Rather than pull out the rug from under these students, we decided to seek private funding to pay their increased tuition costs, which we soon secured. Unfortunately, this did not solve the problem for future students graduating from Arkansas high schools, with the grades and the desire to learn but not the social security numbers, who wanted to enter Arkansas colleges and universities as in-state students.

This episode awakened me to the often heartbreaking lives of undocumented students. It became increasingly clear to me what an impossible situation these young men and women were in—many of whom had been here most of their lives and spoke English with Arkansas accents. They not only had to pay more for college but had to do so without access to financial aid or legal employment, all but condemning them to an underclass existence.

I have also gotten to know several of these nineteen students and many more just like them. They are remarkable kids—intelligent, hard-working, highly motivated, and seeking the same opportunities to better their lives through higher education as the friends they grew up with. Clearly, they are being punished for the crimes of their parents. Their treatment is also a matter of bad public policy. It is a waste of human capital to ensure them access to K–12 education but so completely frustrate their ability to access higher education, all but ensuring their permanent marginalization.

Ultimately, the events of 2008 made me want to learn more about what I could do to help the cause of immigration reform. One of the people I turned to was Bill Schwab, a sociology professor at the University of Arkansas whose research had taken him deep into this subject. Dr. Schwab has been my guide through the changing demographics of our region and has helped educate me on regional and national trends in immigration. He has also helped shape my thinking on the need for immigration reform, particularly the DREAM Act. As the University of Arkansas has striven to create awareness of this issue through various events, Dr. Schwab has been an invaluable resource in dissecting the issues, connecting us with outspoken DREAMers (like the ones profiled here), and providing insight into their lives.

Right to DREAM: Immigration Reform and America's Future is a valuable and important resource in furthering the discussion I unexpectedly joined in 2008. I commend it to you without reservation and in the hopes that it will help shape the thinking of others on this critical issue. Our current immigration policy is clearly broken, and it won't be fixed until more Americans are aware of the issues and options involved.

This book is a great place to start.

G. David Gearhart, Chancellor
University of Arkansas

ACKNOWLEDGMENTS

This book is my fourth. I began working on it in January 2012 and projected a six-month timeline. Like so much in life, other things intervened—new professional responsibilities, my work in Jordan, appreciating my wife and grandchildren, and dealing with the vagaries of life. Now that my work is at a close, I acknowledge those people who aided me along the way.

First, I thank Bob Haslam, the director of the University of Arkansas Quality Writing Center. Bob and I started working together on the Northwest Arkansas Hispanic Community Study in 2007. The relationship between an author and his or her editor is one of trust—editors are sometimes the bearers of bad news. I gave Bob a draft of my first two chapters in January 2012, and we met a few days later for coffee. He put the copy on the table, looked up at me, and said, "Bill, I would love to take this course, but this book is not going to reach your audience—you're writing to academics." Bob is committed to the success of our students and a supporter of the DREAM movement, so I knew that the book had to change. I started over. Thank you, Bob, for your hard work, editing, insightful comments, counsel, and support. It has been an honor working with you these past five years.

Thanks also go to Andy Albertson, a gifted writer and editor, for his comments and suggestions on the manuscript. You helped make this a better book.

Closer to home, thanks go to members of our campus's DREAM movement—Raul Torres, Rocio Aguayo, and Rafael Garcia—who helped frame this book. Special thanks go to Juan Mendez and Zessna Garcia for sharing their stories. Not to be overlooked are the nearly fifty DREAMers who shared their stories through interviews and biographies, as well as the hundreds of DREAMers who allowed me to observe their meetings and hear their stories, hopes, and dreams. I could not have written the book without them.

The University of Arkansas has a remarkable leader in Chancellor G. David Gearhart. His vision of a campus that reflects the diversity of our state is shown in his commitment to the passage of the DREAM Act and comprehensive immigration reform. Without him there would not have been the growth in our campus's diversity, the Undocumented: Living in the Shadows program in April 2012, or this book. Thank you for your support of this project and your commitment to the DREAM movement.

Special thanks go to Larry Malley, director and editor of The University of Arkansas Press, and Brian King, editorial and production director, for the production of this book. I am always amazed at the amount of behind-the-scenes work involved with a book project.

Writing has always been difficult for me, and I have spent years staring at the blank page. My wife, Judy, a gifted writer and a former writing teacher, has helped in my journey as a writer. I will always be her most grateful student. *Voice, unity, coherence,* and all of the other words of her craft now have meaning to me. I thank her for her passion for the written word and her support these past thirty years. Not every author is as fortunate as I am in having a loving and supportive wife and friend.

A book is a collaborative enterprise. Peruse the notes, and find the researchers who contributed to this book. Thanks go to all of them for expanding knowledge of the immigration process, the DREAM movement, and the experiences of undocumented youth. I have tried to faithfully represent their research and stories. If I have fallen short, I alone am responsible.

Right to DREAM

Introduction

Zacatecas, the Nauhatl name for the north-central region of Mexico given by the indigenous people that inhabited the area. It is also the name of the state where I was born twenty-three years ago. It is a place rich with silver mining, as well as colonial history and present-day culture. It is a place I have few memories of and know mostly through books, the Internet, and social media. It is also a place I have not been able to return to since the age of seven. My name is Luis, and I am an undocumented student.

At the age of seven, children don't really think about what is right or wrong. They rely on their parents to guide them and trust they take the actions necessary for a better life. This is exactly what I did when my parents said we were moving to the United States in the pursuit of a better life. The last day of school, my parents were waiting for me outside with backpacks. I became excited with the thought of going on a vacation when, in reality, we were getting on a bus that would take us closer to the Mexican border. Once we got off the bus, we waited for a *coyote*, a man my parents paid a great deal of money to help us cross the border. Our journey took days. We marched on, moving mostly by night, weighed down by worries, bags, and younger siblings. I was too young to understand but old enough to know better than to complain. Our party soon doubled, and we became hungry and tired. All I can remember is a voice whispering in the dark, "Keep walking and stay quiet." A few days later, I was in the United States.

My transition was both easy and hard. I would tell people I met about the adventure we had on our way to the United States head on. It was just like a movie: the danger and suspense unreal in the vivid mind of a young child. For me it simply meant moving to a new place with a nice school, new friends, a new home, and hopefully a new soccer ball. My new home was and is Rogers, Arkansas. My new friends were strangers who could not understand a word that I said except, "I don spek in gleesh," until, after a lot of hard work, I learned the language.

It wasn't until I turned sixteen that I figured out what it really meant to be undocumented. One single event changed my whole life. It took many years to realize what my family and I had done was not an action movie but rather a hard and trying journey, one for which I would not be able to fully reap the benefits. I couldn't share in my friends' joy of getting a driver's license. I couldn't get into rated-R movies with all my friends. I couldn't go back to Mexico to visit the family we left behind, and my dreams of getting a college education were beginning to fade.

After much hard work and more sacrifices, I was able to go on with school. Despite my situation, I was able to save money, attend college, and graduate with an associate's of science in nursing. I was able to graduate from one of the top nursing programs in the state of Arkansas, becoming one of the first Hispanic male nurses to graduate from my school. However, because I am undocumented, I could not (and cannot) work. At the same time, we still have a shortage of nurses in the United States, especially male, bilingual nurses. Since I am not able to get a job, unlike most of my classmates who graduated with me, I have gone back to school and am currently working on getting my bachelor's of science in nursing. I hope that one day my situation can be resolved so I can accomplish my dreams. Not only do I want to work as the emergency room nurse I have always dreamed of being, but I also hold high aspirations to join the military and serve what I now consider to be my country as a military nurse or medic—another one of my dreams that is being put on hold because of the infamous nine-digit number. All I want is to save lives while giving my own life for my country.

An event that happened sixteen years ago has shaped me into what I am today in a positive way. One large event forever changed and altered all my dreams. The one lacking nine-digit number is what builds the barriers I am always trying to break. Every single day, I try to become a better person, live my life as if I had no limitations, and always remember my past in order to reach my future.

These are the words of Luis, one of the nearly fifty young people whom I interviewed or who provided biographies for this book. Though their stories share common themes—parents illegally immigrating to the United States for a better life; arriving as young children and not understanding why; traveling at night through dangerous and inhospitable territory; experiencing hunger, thirst, fear, violence, and sometimes rape; and arriving as a stranger in a strange land, one increasingly hostile to their presence—in my interviews and focus groups I found that they shared other things, as well. They are bright, articulate, and surprisingly optimistic. They attended public schools, learned English, and were socialized as Americans. They have Texas, Oklahoma, and Arkansas accents. Typical teens and young adults, they spend their free time listening to music, hanging out with friends, attending Friday-night games and dances, and worrying about dating and fitting in. Bilingual, they effortlessly navigate between two social worlds. They are family- and church-centered, and most work to help themselves and their families.

When I asked, "Who are you?" they typically answered, "I am an American," or, "I am an American of x heritage." But unlike their classmates, most of them were undocumented and spoke of barriers and blocked opportunities—no driver's licenses when they turned sixteen, no class trips if air travel was required, no part-time jobs if a social security number was needed, and often no college, because they were denied admission, scholarships, or financial aid or could not afford out-of-state tuition.

Some described themselves as Generation 1.5—the undocumented generation, raised as Americans but denied the hope and promise of our nation. At peril of deportation, many came out publicly, declaring their undocumented status, lobbying and marching to highlight the plight of the undocumented, and hoping to change immigration laws.

These are the students I have worked with for the past six years. My interest in their lives began in 2008 when I completed a year-long study on the characteristics and needs of the Hispanic community in northwest Arkansas. The study provided an insight into the impact this population has had on the region and on the institutions, social networks, and political and economic relationships that create and shape it.

As a community sociologist, my basic questions were the following: How do we create a just, fair, and inclusive community? How do we accept a group that is so different from us in culture, religion, and language? How do our institutions—family, health care, education, and religion—assimilate and acculturate our newest residents? How do we take the best of both cultures and create a better community?

I concluded that inclusion was not only what we, as a society, may want to do but something we had to do. The more than 66,000 Hispanics who live in our midst are not going back to where they came from. I know from my research that they have created neighborhoods, rich social networks, and institutions that support their lives, but often in a separate community with very few ties to the larger one. The ties that exist are often formal ones linked to the services they receive in our schools, hospitals, clinics, churches, and chain stores. I concluded that these ties have not brought us together but kept us apart in separate, insulated communities.

I took many things away from my study, but I was left with this troubling feeling that, as a society, we were doing something wrong. Local police departments are partnering with Immigration and Custom Enforcement (ICE) to enforce federal laws. We are creating a climate where skin color is probable cause for a traffic stop or raid on a home, workplace, or apartment. We are deporting parents, forcing them to leave their U.S.-born children behind to be raised by friends, siblings, or other relatives. We are creating a permanent underclass, doing the "immigrant jobs" that no one else will do and, in so doing, condemning millions to the margins of our society. And, for me, the most egregious wrong is punishing children for the behavior of their parents.

There is a common theme—our nation's immigration policy—which most agree is broken. Based on a massive, incoherent, and often contradictory set of laws, the current system does not serve our national interests. Well-educated and skilled workers needed in our high-technology and information-driven industries are denied visas; agriculture workers needed to harvest and process our food are kept from our borders; and the 11 million undocumented living among us live in limbo, existing in an informal economy. Many members of Congress share this view, and immigration reform has been on their legislative agenda for more than a decade. While Republicans call for visa and temporary worker reforms, Democrats demand new naturalization and immigration rules. With a divided government the issue has been a recipe for inaction. Caught in the middle are 2.1 million children and young adults brought here illegally by their parents.

With no consensus on comprehensive immigration reform, a bipartisan group of House and Senate members focused on the future of these undocumented children and young adults. A bill first introduced in 2001 by senators Orrin Hatch (R-UT) and Richard Durbin (D-IL), the Development, Relief, and Education for Alien Minors (DREAM) Act would provide a path to citizenship. The bill is straightforward. If the undocumented youth had entered the United States before age sixteen, lived here for at least five years prior to the legislation's enactment, received a high school degree or GED, and were younger than thirty-five, they could receive conditional immigration status for six years. This would allow them to work, go to school, and travel. After the waiting period, participants could apply for lawful permanent residence. They would have to show they had obtained or pursued a college degree or had honorably served at least two years in the military, as well as maintaining good moral character during their conditional status period. Immigrants who failed to meet these requirements would lose their conditional status and revert to being unauthorized.

The DREAM Act failed in the 107th Congress but has been reintroduced in subsequent sessions as a stand-alone bill or as part of major immigration reform bills. These bills have suffered similar fates. Frustrated with the lack of Congressional action, fourteen states have implemented laws or changed policies that provide educational benefits to undocumented students.[1] While not a fix-all, this stopgap approach has filled the void created by the lack of federal action. As we will see, the state laws were narrowly drawn, providing in-state tuition to undocumented students meeting good faith eligibility requirements, like a diploma from a state high school. Although these laws do not provide a path to citizenship, they do provide a way for undocumented students to get a college degree and contribute to our knowledge-based economy.

This book is about the DREAM Act and the compelling reasons for its passage. It is an extension of my research that began in 2007, and although its focus is on Hispanic students, the law would benefit tens of thousands of undocumented youth who have arrived here from around the world. This book is not just about the DREAM Act, either. There is a lot of social science swirling around this legislation, and my goal is to put the DREAM Act in a social and historical context.

Chapter 1, "These Children Are Blameless," explores the legal issues surrounding the education of immigrant children. The chapter is organized around the Supreme Court's 1982 *Plyler v. Doe* ruling because the issues this case settled thirty years ago are still relevant. Undocumented children are blameless for the violation of immigration law by their parents; education is a prerequisite for full participation in our society; and it is in our national interest that all children, regardless of immigration status, be provided public education. I believe the DREAM Act is a straightforward extension of the *Plyler* principles to the college education of undocumented youth.

Chapter 2, "Immigration 101," looks at the social science research on immigration. I tell the stories of three DREAMers—Rafael, Marco, and Rocio—and explain why their parents moved to the United States. The chapter explores how they were pushed from their hometowns by the lack of opportunity and pulled to the United States by jobs and economic opportunities. I show that those who leave are different from those who stay behind and that immigration is a transfer of wealth from the sending to the receiving society. Opponents argue that many who immigrate here are motivated by educational benefits, but, as I demonstrate, scant evidence exists for this position.

Anti-immigrant groups argue that immigrants are a tax burden, don't pay for the services they use, contribute to state budget shortfalls, and take jobs from American workers. Chapter 3, "Spend a Trillion Dollars a Year and You're a Tax Burden?," looks at the numbers and finds a very different reality. Immigrants grow the economy, create jobs, pay taxes at the federal, state, and local levels, make contributions to Social Security and Medicare, and contribute more in taxes than they cost in social services. They contribute over $1 trillion a year to our economy. One way to look at the DREAM Act is that it is an investment in undocumented youth, an investment that will pay dividends for decades to come.

The nation is amid a fourth wave of immigration, and critics believe that this newest wave is overwhelming American culture. Should we be concerned? Should we pursue drastic measures to stem the tide? Salsa has replaced catsup on our dinner tables, and Chapter 4, "Salsa, America's Number-One Condiment," describes how we have created a pluralistic society by selectively absorbing the culture from each immigrant wave. I argue that this is a process that has enriched, not diminished, American culture. There is another benefit. Our ethnic diversity has created a society tailor-made for the global economy. DREAMers from nations around the world often speak two or more languages and have knowledge of other cultures, global networks, and an entrepreneurial spirit, which are remarkable assets in a global economy and would benefit all of us.

Chapter 5, "The Melting Pot, Mixed with a Few New Ingredients," explores the process of becoming an American, and the research is clear: the newest wave is learning English and assimilating more quickly than the previous ones. And they are successfully pursuing the American Dream. It it important to note that two-thirds of Americans think immigration is a good thing for this country, and an even larger number support the DREAM Act.

Chapter 6, "The DREAM Act: Nuts and Bolts," explores the incoherent, confusing, and often contradictory laws that create our incoherent, confusing, and often contradictory immigration policy. The chapter revisits *Plyler v. Doe,* the Texas court case that set it all in motion. With Congress in gridlock, the states have taken over and passed their own DREAM laws. What do these laws have in common? What are their costs and benefits? Has there been an economic impact? Who and how many undocumented students are eligible? What is the impact on state educational budgets? What are the economic returns on this investment?

Chapter 7, "Meet Two DREAMers," introduces two remarkable undocumented young people, Juan Mendez and Zessna Garcia. Their biographies give authentic voices to the DREAMers' experiences. How did they get to the United States? What were their public school and college experiences? What are the barriers they face? What are the social and psychological costs of being undocumented? How does it feel to live in a mixed-status family? How does the label *undocumented* affect college aspirations? What is the impact of out-of-state tuition? How do undocumented young people manage the fear of deportation? Would kin and friends embrace them if they returned? What do they think of their future? And how would the passage of the DREAM Act change their lives?

The final chapter, "Next Steps: Where We Go from Here," examines growing public support for the DREAM Act and the groundswell of support for the Obama administration's policy for deferred action. It makes the case that it's time for elected officials to stop listening to a vocal minority and begin to address immigration reform in a way that the majority of Americans support. Put simply, it is time to stand up and do the right things: allowing undocumented children and young adults to stay in this country, permitting them to go to school and to seek employment, providing them with a path to citizenship, and giving them the opportunity to contribute to American society.

The 2012 presidential election has changed the playing field. A historic turnout by Hispanic voters (10 percent of the electorate, with 71 percent voting for the president) helped fuel President Obama's re-election. In Nevada, Colorado, and New Mexico, exit polls show that Hispanics were responsible for the margin of victory. In Ohio and Florida, a strong showing from Hispanics and African Americans was a difference-maker. The election has set off Republican soul-searching, and it may very well be a defining moment for immigration reform. Gone from the Republican lexicon are phrases like "self-deportation," replaced with ones like "the need for comprehensive immigration reform." For the first time in a generation, even with a divided Congress, the chances of immigration reform are high. Therefore, the first session of the 113th Congress will be crucial in the immigration reform movement. How can we influence our lawmakers? How can we shape the legislation? Where do we go from here? To help answer these questions, readers are asked to look at our nation's past, particularly the civil rights movement, to revisit the Montgomery bus strike, and to remember the rule of small victories, when the accumulation of small successes leads to major social change. The DREAM movement and the United We Dream Network employ the same organizational principles and a philosophy of nonviolence—the ultimate success of which can be measured by the Department of Homeland Security's new policy of deferred action, which many believe is the first step toward the ultimate passage of the DREAM Act.

Our constitution gives the federal government the power to shape and enforce immigration policy. The majority of Americans think it's time that it does its job. Until they do, it is time that we take the next steps at the state level and pass laws that provide in-state tuition to undocumented youth. Although this approach creates a patchwork of laws, it lays the groundwork and builds momentum for passage of a federal DREAM Act and comprehensive immigration reform. Our democracy is built on ordinary people doing extraordinary things. The book ends with what you can do to get the DREAM Act passed in your state and how you can contribute to a civil civic debate on this nation's immigration policy.

PART I

Answering the Critics

As with other domestic issues, Americans are deeply divided in their beliefs about the long-term effect of our current immigration policy. Some groups, like the Cato Institute, see immigration as a key to a robust and expanding economy, a continuation of the melting pot process that has made America great. Other groups, like the Federation for American Immigration Reform (FAIR), see the rapid increase in racial and ethnic minorities as a threat to America's European heritage. As a result immigration has become this decade's hot-button political issue, not only because of the dramatic increase in the number of immigrants in the past thirty years but also because immigration is the process that defines who we are as a people.

Some Americans feel threatened by these changes. Parties attracted to the immigration debate sometimes respond emotionally when they sense jobs, health care, education, and national security are at risk. In such a charged climate, it is not surprising that Congress has been unable to address comprehensive immigration reform, and the DREAM Act has been at the center of this debate. With no consensus at the national level, states have moved to fill the political vacuum, but state governments are moving in two different directions. On the one hand, fourteen states have decided to improve the opportunities for undocumented students in higher education with the passage of the DREAM Act.[2] On the other, states like Arizona, Alabama, and Florida have passed laws limiting access to higher education for undocumented students, arguing that they are protecting taxpayers.

Landmark social legislation occurs at the confluence of economic, social, and political forces. Historians usually write about the leaders who framed laws and, through the power of their personalities, passed them. In reality, passing landmark legislation requires a Congress who represents an electorate whose attitudes are shaped by the state of the economy and the society and a collective willingness to accept social change. History is replete with examples. President Franklin D. Roosevelt signed the Social Security Act on August 14, 1935. Although controversial, the legislation passed the House 372 to 33, with 81 Republicans voting in support, and the Senate 77 to 6, with 16 Republicans supporting. Thirty years later, President Lyndon B. Johnson signed the Medicare bill into law on July 30, 1965, after passing the House 307 to 116, with 70 Republicans supporting, and the Senate 70 to 24, with 13 Republicans voting for the bill. The same pattern persisted with the Civil Rights Act of 1964 and the Voting Rights Act of 1965. Were they controversial? Yes. Were they products of their times? Yes. Can the vast majority of Americans conceive of a society without Social Security and Medicare? Probably not. Most appreciate the role these laws have played in creating a civil society. But ask yourself, "Would any of these bills pass Congress today? Would there be an attempt to cross the aisle, compromise, and vote for what was good for the nation? Would the majority of Congress cast a vote for the *common good*?"

The 2012 presidential election was a game-changer. Congressional Republicans have stalled immigration reform and the DREAM Act for a decade, but the growing share of Hispanic voters, which helped re-elect the president, is likely to double by 2030. Heeding the warning, prominent Republicans are launching a new super-PAC, Republicans for Immigration Reform, with the hope of repairing the political damage left by years of anti-immigrant rhetoric. Political relevance, not the common good, is driving these efforts, but it is creating the best chance for comprehensive immigration reform in a generation. But words are cheap, and the American people should not be surprised if Congress cannot pass a comprehensive immigration reform bill. This is why the states must continue to provide leadership on this issue.

In the next five chapters, I explore the key issues surrounding passage of the DREAM Act. What are the issues that divide? What do the proponents and opponents of the DREAM Act argue? Is there a middle ground? Is compromise possible? As with all controversial legislation, arguments on both sides abound. I believe the following five arguments are the ones most commonly and most forcefully set forth by opponents of the DREAM Act:

> *Legal.* Undocumented students are criminals. They are breaking the law. Passing the DREAM Act would reward criminals by extending higher education to undocumented students. The criminals should go home, get in line, and apply to enter the country legally.

> *Immigration.* Passing the DREAM Act would lure more illegal immigrants to the United States. More families would attempt illegal entry so that their children could receive an education and attain legal status. The DREAM Act would cause an increase in illegal immigration.

> *Economic.* Undocumented residents are a tax burden. They consume services and do not pay their way. They exacerbate state budget shortfalls in a time of recession. Trapped in low-paying "immigrant jobs," they contribute little to the economy and less to the tax base.

> *Culture.* They are changing our national character. We are a white, Christian nation grounded in a European heritage.

> *Assimilation.* Undocumented immigrants will not be a part of the melting pot, because they live in insular, non-English-speaking communities bound by networks of kin and friends.

ONE

These Children Are Blameless

Legal. Undocumented students are criminals. They are breaking the law. Passing the DREAM Act would reward criminals by extending higher education to undocumented students. The criminals should go home, get in line, and apply to enter the country legally.

The critics of the DREAM Act argue that Congress twice clearly stated the nation's position on illegal immigration during the Clinton administration by passing the Personal Responsibility and Work Opportunity Reconciliation Act of 1996 (PRWORA) and the Illegal Immigrant Reform and Immigration Responsibility Act (IIRIRA). These laws addressed several immigration concerns of that time: removing incentives for illegal immigration, limiting benefits to those who were here illegally, and barring illegal immigrants' employment in highly skilled jobs.[1]

The critics also note that in their 1982 ruling in *Plyler v. Doe,* the Supreme Court distinguished undocumented children from adults who illegally came to the United States, and their ruling required states to provide K–12 education to undocumented children. In IIRIRA, Congress codified the distinction between children and their parents, and because the court did not extend educational benefits beyond primary and secondary education, once children reached eighteen the law required them to correct their undocumented status. In other rulings the court recognized that illegal residents in the United States enjoyed protection of their fundamental rights under the Constitution, but opponents note the court did not classify education as a fundamental right.

The critics also argue that the DREAM Act would negatively impact the nation's immigration policy. First, they claim that the act would discourage young adults who have reached the age of eighteen from correcting their illegal status. Second, state DREAM Acts would circumvent Congress's ability to control the immigration and naturalization process. And third, giving undocumented students in-state tuition benefits would reward illegal behavior and give undocumented students preferential treatment. Moreover, they note, IIRIRA does not bar undocumented students from higher education; rather, it requires them to pay out-of-state tuition.[2]

First, I will put the DREAM Act in a legal context. In 1982 the Supreme Court held in *Plyler v. Doe* that Texas violated the Equal Protection Clause of the Fourteenth Amendment by denying undocumented school-age children a free public education. Justice William J. Brennan wrote for the majority, and his words are as relevant today as they were thirty years ago.[3]

Justice Brennan notes that because of lax enforcement and our unwillingness to bar the employment of the undocumented, our society had created a "shadow population" of illegal immigrants, numbering in the millions. Little has changed in three decades—today, the nation has 11.2 million undocumented residents, including 2.1 million children and young adults.

Justice Brennan continues, "The existence of such an underclass presents most difficult problems for a Nation that prides itself on adherence to principles of equality under law." He notes that adults who enter our territory illegally should be "prepared to bear the consequences, including, but not limited to, deportation." But he makes an important distinction in that "the children of those illegal entrants are not comparably situated." Simply, children are not responsible for the behavior of their parents; they represent a special case.

Justice Brennan then describes the special role of education in our society as follows: "In addition to the pivotal role of education in sustaining our political and cultural heritage, denial of education to some isolated group of children poses an affront to one of the goals of the Equal Protection Clause: the abolition of governmental barriers presenting unreasonable obstacles to advancement on the basis of individual merit." So this right of individual advancement is protected by our Constitution, and it remains, after more than two hundred years, a core American value. We are a meritocracy.

Justice Brennan concludes:

Paradoxically, by depriving the children of any disfavored group of an education, we foreclose the means by which that group might raise the level of esteem in which it is held by the majority.... The inability to read and write will handicap the individual deprived of a basic education each and every day of his life. The inestimable toll of that deprivation on the social, economic, intellectual, and psychological wellbeing of the individual, and the obstacle it poses to individual achievement, make it most difficult to reconcile the cost or the principle of a status-based denial of basic education with the framework of equality embodied in the Equal Protection Clause.

Justice Brennan reasons that without the basic skills education provides, these undocumented children would become part of a permanent underclass. Consequently, the court ruled that undocumented children were entitled to the same K–12 education that the state provided children whose parents were citizens. But the law did not extend this guarantee to postsecondary education.

I believe the principles identified in *Plyler v. Doe* are as relevant today as when they were written. Education is indispensable to our society. It is the foundation of our democracy. It contributes to the common good. It is necessary for meaningful participation in our economy and society, and it is the major contributor to upward social mobility. It is doubtful that any child could succeed in our society if denied the opportunity of an education.

But much has changed in our society and economy in the past thirty years. We are no longer an industrial society but a postindustrial one. We still make things, but products from our knowledge- and information-based economy have eclipsed those from manufacturing. When students graduated from high school or college thirty years ago, they competed with graduates from their communities, states, and region. Today, with the mixed blessings of the Internet, graduates compete with millions of others worldwide. In the recent past a high school education and a union job helped to ensure a middle-class lifestyle. With the collapse of unions and the rise of a global economy, a high school education alone would keep someone at the margins of our society. So a K–12 education was to the twentieth century what a K–16 education is to the twenty-first.

Our Constitution and laws are living documents, and as our society has changed our Congress, our states' legislatures, and our courts have created a legal system that has served the needs of each generation of Americans. Our nation must now recognize that we are amid the fourth great wave of immigration in our history, and, as in the past, this wave will reinvigorate and change us. In *Plyler v. Doe,* Justice Brennan recognizes the necessity to educate undocumented children in order to help prevent their exile to the permanent underclass, and it is vital that our generation recognizes that 2.1 million young people require more than a K–12 education. They need a higher education in order to avoid the exile Brennan argues against.

The critics of the DREAM Act argue that it would discourage young adults who have reached the age of eighteen from correcting their illegal status and claim that without the act an undocumented youth, in order to gain legal status, need only return to her or his native country, apply for legal admission to the United States, and get in line for a visa. Framing the argument differently, these critics want us to educate undocumented children; to allow them to make friends, attend public schools, participate in their communities, and become Americans, except for their immigration status; and then, when they turn eighteen, to deport them. Are these young people any more culpable for their parents' actions after they reach the age of majority at eighteen? A growing number of Americans think not.

I have conducted interviews and focus groups with undocumented students, ESL teachers, school administrators, and governmental officials; I have attended regional and state DREAM Act conferences; and I have learned that the go-home-and-get-in-line position ignores reality. First, is it a reasonable alternative? Would an undocumented youth who returned be able to get a visa in, say, a year or two? The answer is no. The U.S. immigration process is chaotic, time-consuming, and expensive. At the end of 2010, 1,381,896 Mexicans (the source of 60 percent of our immigration) were still waiting for their green card applications to be accepted or rejected. The United States currently makes only 5,000 green cards annually available worldwide for low-wage workers to immigrate permanently; in recent years only a few of those have gone to Mexicans.[4] The reality is that an undocumented youth could not leave, return legally, and restart life in the United States. The majority of young adults that I interviewed knew this and lived in constant fear of being stopped, arrested, detained, and deported. When I talked to them, they said that the fear was always just below the surface, and the fear was palpable in my interviews, usually accompanied by tears. In one of my focus groups with undocumented students, one-third were being treated for depression because of this underlying fear.

How could it be otherwise? These young people have been raised, educated, and socialized as Americans. English is their first language, and their hopes, values, and beliefs are American. When I explored their lifestyles, I found that what they wore, listened to, and admired came from American popular culture. They share our language and culture, and yes, they have rich networks of family, friends, and neighbors. But those networks are here.

Critics argue, however, that these young adults would be fine if they were to go back to their native countries—that they would have kin, friends, and neighbors to support them. In my research I found the opposite to be true. Most of these young people came to the United States at a very young age and have little or no memory of the family and neighbors in their native country. With increased border security, return trips for visits and holidays are impossible. Their parents keep relationships alive through international phone calls, but these are not ties that bind a younger generation. Therefore, most of these young people, if deported, would be strangers in a strange land.

Another wrinkle in the opponents' argument is little known or appreciated. About one-third of the students I interviewed were from mixed-status families. For example, Carlos, whom I interviewed at a District 8 United We Dream conference, was brought by his parents to the United States for medical treatment when he was two months old.[5] He would have died in Mexico, but the hospital stay in Kansas City saved his life. His parents overstayed their visa, joined Kansas City's Latino community, and worked in the underground economy to support their family.

Today, his parents have permanent residency, and his younger siblings are citizens because they were born here. Carlos is the only undocumented member of his family. He has never met his Mexican kin, has talked to them only a few times, and became visibly upset when the subject of deportation was brought up. Carlos told me:

I'm an American. There were only two other Latinos in my high school. I know where I came from, uh, I know I'm Latino. . . . I just think of myself as . . . like I belong here . . . this is my country . . . right? Do you understand me? I played football and basketball in high school. I'm a good student. High school was incredible. The teachers and kids were great to me. I really did well. I really belonged. Great years. It was great. The guys I played sports with and my girlfriend Allison, you know, Allison and her friends, were my group. We've been together since the ninth grade; that's my group. . . . Allison's parents . . . they treat me like I'm a member of the family. They don't know that I'm undocumented. They think I'm American.

I asked him, "When did your parents tell you you were undocumented?" I was astounded to learn they told him when he wanted to get a driver's license. He had no idea there was a problem.

He said, "They didn't tell me, because they didn't want it getting out they were here illegally. They're legal now."

What troubles him most is how easy his younger brothers have it. They have cars, driver's licenses, and financial aid for college. Carlos works for cash, drives without a license but buys insurance, and struggles from semester to semester to raise money for tuition. At the end of our interview, I discovered another wrinkle in the argument from the critics. I asked him, "How's your Spanish?"

He said, "I'm fluent but learned it at home." He took two years in high school, thinking it would be an easy A, but it wasn't.

He said, "I speak village Spanish at home. . . . Formal Spanish is different. I can speak it, read it okay, but I'd never get a job in Mexico."

My interview with Jeannette, the former cultural liaison officer for a local school district, gave me additional insight into the language challenges these young people face. She reminded me that many of their parents were from villages and small towns in Mexico and Central and South America, that they did not speak standard Spanish, and that many were illiterate. She went on to say that the high school students with whom she worked learned household Spanish and that most neither read nor wrote the language. The following is a profile of a young person whom we would deport: foreign-born, brought here at a young age, educated K–12 in U.S. schools, and supported in ethnic neighborhoods during formative years. Although these students are, at home, shaped by the food, religion, and family customs of their native countries, the powerful norming influence of public education and their Anglo peers in the classroom and the lunchroom and on the playing field has socialized them as Americans. The idea that they would thrive in their native countries thus is dubious because they lack the social networks, language and communication skills, and knowledge of the culture necessary to succeed.

Jeannette raised another issue facing these young people. Since schools have pushed for no Spanish to be spoken at home—believing it would force parents and children to learn English—some immigrant children have trouble communicating with their parents in either English or Spanish. In some cases the school brings interpreters to parent-teacher conferences in order to translate within the family. And we would deport these young people?

What if the critics got their way? What if we deported 2.1 million undocumented children on their eighteenth birthdays? What if young adults returned to their native countries and applied for legal immigration to the United States? What would happen while they waited? Would they work? Would they thrive in the villages, neighborhoods, and cities their parents left decades ago? These questions have not been thoroughly explored, but a partial answer comes from my Internet interviews with Rocio.

Rocio was undocumented. Her parents illegally came to northwest Arkansas when she was four. She was educated in the Springdale public schools, and she received her bachelor's degree from the University of Arkansas. The recession hit the family hard, and they decided to return to Mexico. Her parents told her things had gotten much better in Mexico since their leaving twenty years earlier.

Rocio is college-educated, with a degree in marketing, and is fluent in two languages. She has been unemployed for the past two years, however, because she does not have the necessary paperwork to work in Mexico, and she cannot work in the United States, because she is undocumented. The family has hired an immigration specialist, but he says it will take at least a decade for reentry, if ever. What broke my heart was when she told me, "I just don't fit in." She lives with her parents, and her life revolves around family and kin. She has not made good friends in her community—her friends are in Arkansas—and she is homesick. She misses her friends and the rhythm of her life in Springdale. She is under a doctor's care for depression because Rocio is a woman without a country.

Critics of the DREAM Act argue that it would take away any incentive for undocumented students to change their immigration status. First, these students are Americans, different only in immigration status. Their formative years were spent here; their family and friends live here; and since most came at a young age, they have little or no memory of their lives in another country. Do critics really believe that these young people would voluntarily leave their homes and move to a country they do not know in the distant hope of returning and receiving educational benefits? The rational decision would be to stay here and face the specter of deportation. Second, because children under eighteen possess the immigration status of their parents and they inherit this status when they come of age, young adults have little chance in gaining legal status under current immigration law—unless their parents can obtain it—so the odds of gaining reentry are slim if they leave.

Thus, the DREAM Act is a recognition of the legal limbo in which undocumented students find themselves. The act acknowledges the reality that few undocumented students would voluntarily leave this country to change their immigration status. Further, it acknowledges that students have built communities in the United States and that if they left this country, they likely would never be able to return and that if they did return in a decade or two, the world they left would no longer be here. Their friends would have moved on in life, and their networks would be scattered. Punishing these young people for an act they did not commit is not going to have the desired effect. The DREAM Act does not reward anyone; the act simply is humane.

Critics of the DREAM Act also argue that when states pass their own DREAM Acts, they circumvent Congress's ability to control the immigration and naturalization process. Immigration data suggest, however, the opposite. Take Mexico, the largest source of immigrants to the United States, as an example. Douglas S. Masey, codirector of the Mexican Migration Project at Princeton, reports that interest among young Mexicans in immigrating to the United States has fallen to the lowest level since the 1950s. Professor Massey states in a July 6, 2011,

New York Times interview that "no one wants to hear it, but the flow has already stopped. For the first time in 60 years, the net traffic has gone to zero and is probably a little bit negative."[6]

The decline in illegal immigration from a country responsible for 60 percent of the nation's estimated 11 million illegal immigrants has been stark. Mexico's 2010 census discovered 4 million more citizens than projected, reflecting a sharp decline in immigration to the United States. And the Pew Hispanic Center reports similar findings. They found the flow of illegal Mexicans to the United States shrank to fewer than 100,000 in 2010, down from an estimated 525,000 just a decade ago.[7]

It appears that federal efforts to control illegal immigration have been successful, and state laws have not circumvented the federal government's ability to control immigration. Increased border security, ICE's vigorous enforcement of our laws, and a record number of deportations by the Obama administration has had the desired effect. When federal efforts are combined with a deep recession; a steep decline in immigrant jobs in agriculture, construction, and service; and the passage of anti-immigrant laws in Arizona, Alabama, Florida, and other states, the decision-making calculus of possible immigrants has changed. The United States no longer is a desirable destination for jobs or a better life. Not to be overlooked are Mexico's investments in family planning, health care, and education, which have expanded the nation's economic opportunities. The opportunities in the United States that have pulled immigrants here for the past thirty years have ended, and the Mexican government's efforts to reduce the push factors by increasing the nation's educational and economic opportunities have stopped most illegal immigration across our southern border. Therefore, this new reality means that the immigration debate needs to shift from policies designed to stop the flow of illegals to ones that address the plight of those already here, especially the 2.1 million undocumented children and young people who live among us.

Another of the critics' arguments is that giving undocumented students in-state tuition benefits rewards illegal behavior and gives undocumented students preferential treatment. They note that federal laws do not bar undocumented students from higher education; rather, they require the undocumented to pay out-of-state tuition.[8]

Implicit in this argument is a need for punishment—illegal behavior should have consequences. Although punishment is not the explicit goal of IIRIRA, undocumented students are labeled lawbreakers in the statute and must change their immigration status when they turn eighteen to receive educational benefits.

Thirty years ago, the Supreme Court recognized that undocumented children do not have culpability for their parent's behavior—a child cannot voluntarily violate immigration law. But federal law labels them as lawbreakers when they turn eighteen. To put this in another context, would people want our courts to punish the children of a drug dealer for his or her crimes? I believe most people would say no, that these children were blameless. Would we want to punish them for their parent's drug crime when they turned eighteen? Again, to most people this question would seem absurd. Why then would it be different for a child whose parents' actions left them with an undocumented status? The children did not commit the act, but they are nonetheless labeled as lawbreakers when they turn eighteen. Although *Plyler v. Doe* recognizes that they are not culpable, under IIRIRA they inherit the immigration status of their parents when they turn eighteen. And here's the rub. Unless their parents can gain legal status, young adults have little chance of changing theirs under current immigration law. Although limiting access to higher education is not punishment in a traditional legal sense (the state is not jailing or fining them), it nonetheless is punishment, because it denies them the opportunities and jobs that higher education provides. This loss is reflected in recent census data. In 2010 the average annual income of a high school graduate was $35,035, and that of a college graduate was $55,864, a difference of over $900,000 in lifetime earnings.[9]

Finally, critics argue that under current federal law, these students can go to school—they just have to pay out-of-state tuition. In Arkansas, however, in-state tuition in 2011–12 was $5,888, and out-of-state tuition was $16,321.[10] Since most undocumented students come from low-income families, these laws effectively bar their access to a higher education. When you combine tuition costs with no financial aid and few work options, owing to legal status, most undocumented youth cannot afford college. And those who do earn a degree face the additional obstacle of being unable to work legally. So there is a dismal future for the approximately 65,000 undocumented students who will graduate from the nation's high schools this year, and the nation is depriving itself of these students' skills and talents.

As I have shown, the critics of the DREAM Act argue that passage would negatively impact the nation's immigration policy by discouraging young adults from correcting their illegal status, circumventing Congress's ability to control the immigration and naturalization process, and rewarding illegal behavior by giving undocumented students in-state rather than out-of-state tuition. These arguments do not stand scrutiny.

More than thirty years ago, the Supreme Court ruled in *Plyler v. Doe* that undocumented children were blameless for the violation of immigration law by their parents. Laws passed in the 1990s, however, labeled them lawbreakers when they turned eighteen. My research has shown that, under current law, changing the immigration status inherited from their parents is, for all intents and purposes, impossible. Undocumented youth are Americans in all but their immigration status because we have raised them this way, and returning them to their country of origin is unreasonable, unrealistic, and inhumane. These young adults will not voluntarily move to a country they do not know in order to possibly receive educational benefits down the road. Instead, they will stay here and face deportation. The national immigration debate must change because federal law enforcement has been effective—illegal immigration across our southern border has stopped. It is time to focus this discussion on what to do with the 2.1 million undocumented children and young adults who live among us. Policy must balance the needs of society with the humane treatment of these people. It should also acknowledge that we have already invested in their education and upbringing and that it is time we use this human capital. The DREAM Acts passed by fourteen states give undocumented students who have graduated a state's high school in-state college tuition. It is a first step, one that can build momentum for the passage of a federal DREAM Act that combines the ability to attend college with legal permanent residency and a path to citizenship.

TWO

Immigration 101

Immigration. Passing the DREAM Act would lure more illegal immigrants to the United States. More families would attempt illegal entry so that their children could receive an education and attain legal status. The DREAM Act would cause an increase in illegal immigration.

In this chapter I show that the overwhelming majority of the families who currently cross our borders come for immediate economic gain and that passage of the DREAM Act would not enter into their decision to immigrate to the United States. I have gained a better understanding of the immigration process from my research on northwest Arkansas's Hispanic community. My work with this community began in 2007, and in 2011 I focused my research on its undocumented children and young adults. I have interviewed and collected biographies on forty-nine undocumented youth and have conducted focus groups and observed the meetings of local organizations. Three of my subjects, Rafael, Marco, and Rocio, are representatives of my sample.

Rafael was born in Moroleón, an industrial town in south-central Mexico, and lived there until he was three years old. He and his parents arrived in Los Angeles on May 5, 1990, a date he remembers because it was Cinco de Mayo. The family's social network was crucial in the move. Family in the United States provided the information and contacts for a safe border crossing. Soon after the crossing, Rafael and his parents joined his uncle, aunt, and three cousins in Los Angeles and shared a one-room trailer for the first year, until his parents could find work and their own place. Rafael says that his parents came to the United States for work because few opportunities were available in their hometown and that they planned to stay only two years, until they saved enough money to go back and start a better life in Mexico.

Thirteen years later, the family was still here, and Rafael was entering high school. He says that going to college was never discussed at home—the expectation was that he would get a job after graduation and contribute to the family's income. His teachers in junior high and high school "preached the idea of college," but "it was something that [Rafael] put away in the backburner." Rafael knew he was undocumented, but he did not fully appreciate how his status would affect his college plans. He writes, "I always figured I would go to college, but how? That, I did not know."

Rafael goes on to explain:

> In California the undocumented are privileged to pay for in-state tuition. A fact I would not learn about until my second semester at California State University Dominguez Hills. My first semester I paid for out-of-state tuition being completely unaware that the California bill, AB-540, gave me the right to pay for in-state tuition. I learned about this half way in to paying off my second semester through the daughter of one of my mother's coworkers. . . . Those first two semesters were incredibly stressful for my family and me. My parents' savings were practically gone and their job earnings combined with mine [would] not cover the out-of-state tuition much longer. I saw the prideful look in my parents' eyes not wanting to admit and state that I would not be able to attend school anymore because we could not afford it. Thankfully, I found out about the AB-540 bill in time, otherwise another might have been the story.

The lack of opportunity in Moroleón and the promise of higher wages in Southern California—i.e., economic factors—clearly provided the impetus for Raphael's family to migrate. Social scientists study why people move, how people move, and who goes where and in what numbers. Although social scientists do not completely understand the complex set of economic, cultural, social, and psychological factors that influence international migration, scientists do agree on four broad factors that drive migration: push factors, pull factors, social networks, and intervening barriers.

Push factors include wars, famines, natural disasters, and authoritarian or corrupt governments that sometimes give migrants a stark choice: stay and die or migrate and live. But research has shown that poor living conditions, financial hardship, low wages, high unemployment, lack of investment opportunities, and misguided government policies that disrupt traditional markets and agricultural communities are more common factors. Together, they create a climate where citizens begin to look for opportunities abroad.

Social scientists describe pull factors as forces present in countries with stable governments and the rule of law. These countries offer the promise of jobs, economic opportunities, safety, and a higher quality of life for immigrants and their families. Together, these forces encourage immigration. Wage differences can be enormous, even in low-skill jobs. For example, agricultural labor in the United States pays twenty times more than comparable work in Mexico and Central America.

Raphael's family immigrated to the United States in what social scientists would describe as a push-pull model. Financial hardship at home drove the family across the border, where economic opportunities (jobs and wages) were dramatically better. Educational benefits were not a part of the decision-making calculus of his parents. The family's chances for a successful crossing were increased through their transnational social network, and kin provided a place to live and information on the local job market.

The connections available to Rafael's family are an example of social networks, the third factor driving immigration. Social networks based in kinship, friendship, and shared hometowns link immigrants and potential immigrants. The first generation of immigrants creates networks in the new society, and once networks are established and connections are made between sending and receiving communities, the risks associated with immigration fall. Social networks are extremely important in understanding the nation's immigration, especially from Mexico and Central America.

All of the individuals introduced in this chapter and throughout the book confronted what social scientists describe as the fourth major factor affecting immigration: *barriers,* which include cost, distance, and the destination countries' immigration policies and their enforcement. In the 1990s and early 2000s, the costs and risks of entering the United

States across the southern border were low, and the number of illegal immigrants in the United States swelled to 12 million. After 9/11, immigration patterns changed: the United States built its Mexican border fence and increased enforcement. Most illegal immigration ended by 2011.

Marco was born in Ario de Rosales in the southwestern Mexican state of Michoacán. His family was already in the United States, so they arranged for him to be smuggled across the border to join his mother. He was fourteen.

Marco remembers traveling to the border with a younger boy, the smuggler, and a driver. He was anxious because his mother had told him of her harrowing seven-day border crossing. But being the oldest child, he was brave because he wanted to show the younger boy everything was going to be OK.

A few hours after leaving his hometown, they pulled up to a bridge on the Texas border. The driver stopped, and the boys jumped out and crawled along the bridge's walkway. Safely across, they squeezed through a hole in the border fence. They were in the United States.

Running from the border, they soon found themselves in the middle of a sugarcane field. The cane's sharp leaves whipped at their arms, and when the younger boy fell behind, Marco protectively put him in back. Exhausted and covered in cuts, they finally reached the highway, where the smuggler was waiting for them. They drove to Hidalgo, Texas, and a few days later, Marco was reunited with his mother in Green Forest, Arkansas.

With few economic opportunities in Mexico, Marco's mother had moved to Green Forest for work in a local poultry plant, a job she had learned about through hometown friends who had moved north a few years earlier. With a secure job and roots in the town's Hispanic neighborhood, she soon saved enough to bring Marco to her. Marco arrived in Arkansas with a new home, new friends, and within days a new school, Green Forest High School. He spoke no English, but with the help of dedicated teachers, he learned English in a few months and did well in school.

Once again, the motivation for immigration was economic, and the family's transnational social network reduced the risks associated with the migration and cushioned the financial and social risks in

Arkansas. Educational benefits were *not* a part of his parents' decision-making process. But Marco is bright and driven. Encouraged by his teachers and mother, he worked and saved after high school and attended the University of Arkansas, graduating in 2010. Marco is fortunate because he has secured his green card and works as a professional in northwest Arkansas.

Rocio moved to Springdale, Arkansas from Guadalajara when she was seven years old. She has few memories of Mexico but knows that they were very poor, to the point that her brothers could not finish school, because they had to help her father work and provide for the family. Her mother had a lot of relatives in Arkansas, so her "three older brothers decided they wanted to come over here and see what they could do for themselves." This was in 1997. Her mother was the care provider for her grandfather. Rocio remarks, "[When] he finally passed away, we didn't have anything to keep us there at all. . . . We just decided it was the time to move. The rest of us came over here with my grandma."

They traveled by bus from Guadalajara to Mexicali, the town across the border from Calexico, California. They had a harrowing bus trip, but once they were in Mexicali, they hired a *coyote,* waited until dark, and made the crossing. Rocio still remembers crossing but doesn't remember the fear. "Like, I was really small, and so I remember just kind of hopping and skipping along with my sister. It was really beautiful, actually, because there's no light and so we could see all the shooting stars." Once in the United States, they hired cabs and drove to a house rented by her grandmother. They spent the weekend there waiting for her cousin to arrive from Arkansas in order to drive them to their new home in Springdale. Arriving in Arkansas, they moved in with her brothers until her parents could find jobs and a house of their own. As in the stories of Rafael and Marco, a lack of opportunity pushed them out of Guadalajara, and the promise of jobs and a better life pulled them to Arkansas. Social networks were crucial in crossing the border and penetrating the financial and social barriers upon their arrival in Springdale.

The stories of all but four of the young people in my study share themes similar to those in Rafael's, Marco's, and Rocio's. First, the motivation for emigrating from the various origin countries of the young people in my study—Mexico, those in Central and South America, and Pakistan, Ghana, and Vietnam—was economic. Few opportunities existed in the sending countries, and their families hoped for jobs and a better quality of life in the United States. In only four cases were medical care and family reunification motivators.

Second, in most cases immigration was viewed as a short-term solution to financial distress in their sending country. Jobs in the informal economy were plentiful in northwest Arkansas, and parents planned to work for a few years before returning home. In the past going north for work in one's teens and twenties was viewed as a rite of passage for young people in Mexico and Central America. In addition, husbands would pursue seasonal work in the states, save, and return to their families in the off-season. One of the unintended consequences of militarizing our southern border has, therefore, been to change seasonal migration into permanent immigration.

Third, these changes in immigration policy were reflected in the experiences of my sample. Almost one-quarter of the young people were part of a pattern called *serial migration*. Fathers and mothers would immigrate first, leaving children behind to be raised by grandparents and relatives. Only when parents were established in their new communities did the children follow. Research shows that serial immigration and the separation of families have serious social and psychological costs for children.[1]

Fourth and finally, in not a single case were K–12 or higher-education benefits a factor in parents' decision-making calculus. Parents were pushed out of their country of origin by poverty and the lack of opportunity and were drawn to the United States for jobs in the agriculture, construction, and service sectors. Why would it be otherwise? Even in a best-case scenario, college and in-state educational benefits for children would be a decade or more in the future. Simply put, these young people were brought to the United States by their parents, and the parents came in search of better jobs with better pay.

Though the DREAM Act's critics argue that we should not allow undocumented immigrants to add a financial burden to our states' universities and colleges, the irony is that state-supported colleges and universities would gain from granting in-state tuition to undocumented immigrants. Studies in California, Massachusetts, North Carolina, and

Texas reveal that if those states allowed undocumented immigrants to attend college at in-state tuition rates, their institutions would gain millions in new tuition income. The argument is all the more compelling when we consider that admissions offices are seeing the tail end of the millennial generation. Over the next decade the number of high school graduates will decline, and higher education, for the first time in over a decade, will face falling enrollments. Colleges and universities could accommodate this small number of additional students—nationally, DREAMers would amount to 65,000 students per year—at little added cost while improving their bottom lines. Some states currently allow the undocumented to attend but require them to pay out-of-state tuition. Some argue that these states would lose revenue by allowing the undocumented to pay the reduced in-state tuition rate. A Massachusetts study shows this assumption to be faulty because most DREAMers are priced out of higher education when forced to pay out-of-state tuition and, thus, the state loses possible in-state tuition and, therefore, revenue.[2]

Passing the DREAM Act therefore would not entice immigrant families to move to the United States so that their children could receive an education and attain legal status. The students I introduce in this chapter, Rafael, Marco, and Rocio, all belong to families who came to the United States for reasons that had no connection to education. As I have shown, immigrants are pushed out of their countries of origin by the lack of economic opportunities and pulled to the United States for jobs. In the short run the DREAM Act would allow colleges and universities to earn more money by tapping underused capacity. In the long run each dollar spent on tuition would result in a $4.20 return in income taxes over the working lives of these young people. From a purely economic standpoint, college and universities and the states themselves have a lot to lose by denying in-state tuition to undocumented students.[3]

THREE

Spend a Trillion Dollars a Year and You Are a Tax Burden?

Economic. Undocumented residents are a tax burden. They consume services and do not pay their way. They exacerbate state budget shortfalls in a time of recession. Trapped in low-paying "immigrant jobs," they contribute little to the economy and less to the tax base.

The Federation for American Immigration Reform (FAIR), a conservative advocacy group that favors tougher immigration laws, contends that illegal aliens cost U.S. taxpayers more than $100 billion each year. Jack Martin, director of special projects for FAIR, believes "undocumented workers leave taxpayers with a fat bill, considering that the government spends money on the workers, and they almost never pay income taxes." He argues, "More forceful implementation of immigration laws could save each U.S. household in the neighborhood of a couple of thousand dollars a year." Martin acknowledges that the $100 billion deficit is a rough estimate. He claims to have arrived at the calculation by subtracting governmental outlays for education, health care, and other benefits from property, sales, and income taxes collected from illegal workers. Still, he insists the findings are clear—illegal immigrants are a drain on state budgets. One of his major points is that "more than half of the country's illegal immigrants work in the 'underground economy' earning cash wages and paying no taxes." Martin further protests that immigrants "take entry-level jobs from Americans."[1]

So are FAIR and other anti-immigration groups right? Are undocumented residents a tax burden? Do they pay for the services they use? Do they contribute to state budget shortfalls? Do they take jobs away from American workers? Do immigrants harm the U.S. economy? Let's take a closer look.

Taxes

Ernesto Zedillo, former president of Mexico and current director of the Yale Center for the Study of Globalization, says that illegal immigrants are a drain on government services only when they are *prevented* from paying taxes.[2] For example, a Social Security number is required for an individual return, but the IRS reports that 6 million people file tax returns each year using an Individual Taxpayer Identification Number (ITIN)—most are undocumented residents. Similarly, the Congressional Budget Office estimates that 50 to 75 percent of unauthorized immigrants pay federal, state, and local taxes, including $7 billion each year in Social Security taxes.[3]

What about taxes paid at the state and local levels? The Immigration Policy Center estimates that households headed by unauthorized immigrants paid $11.2 billion in state and local taxes in 2010. This figure includes $1.2 billion in personal income taxes, $1.6 billion in property taxes, and $8.4 billion in sales taxes. In spite of their undocumented status, these immigrants are adding value to the U.S. economy as workers, as consumers, as business owners, and, of course, as taxpayers.[4]

Data collected at the state level provide additional evidence that undocumented workers make significant contributions to government accounts. The Oregon Center for Public Policy found that their state's undocumented population (estimated at 125,000 to 175,000) contributes $1.8 to $2.5 billion to Oregon's economy. In addition, the undocumented contribute between $65 and $90 million in property, state income, and excise taxes. This estimate does not include the $56 to $79 million annually contributed to Social Security and the $13 to $18 million paid in Medicare taxes. And employers must match their employees' Social Security and Medicare taxes. Ineligible for benefits, many undocumented workers in fact are helping to fund the Social Security and Medicare benefits of older Americans and paying into a system from which they will never collect. The Oregon Center found that, overall, undocumented residents paid more in taxes than they received in benefits.[5]

An Arkansas study commissioned by the Winthrop Rockefeller Foundation in 2007 found the state's documented and undocumented immigrants paid an annual total of $257 million in sales, income, property, and business and personal taxes. The state spent only $237 million, however, delivering services (education, health, and corrections) to the immigrant population. The state netted $19.5 million. The study also projected the consumer spending of immigrants would contribute $5.2 billion to the Arkansas economy by 2010, and their spending would help create 87,000 new jobs. Focusing only on undocumented immigration, a 2012 report by the Institute for Taxation and Economic Policy found that unauthorized immigrants in Arkansas paid $73.3 million in state and local taxes in 2010, including $11 million in state income taxes, $3 million in property taxes, and $59.4 million in sales taxes. These data do not include their contributions to Social Security, Medicare, and unemployment programs, from which they receive no benefits.[6]

How could FAIR and other anti-immigration groups have gotten it so wrong? One error was counting people who were not undocumented. Walter Ewing, a senior researcher at the American Immigration Council, writes, "The single biggest 'expense' [FAIR] attributes to unauthorized immigrants is the education of their children, yet most of these children are native-born, U.S. citizens who will grow up to be taxpaying adults." He continues, "It is disingenuous to count the cost of investing in the education of these children, so that they will earn higher incomes and pay more in taxes when they are adults, as if it were nothing more than a cost incurred by their parents." He added that "the report fails to account for the purchasing power of unauthorized consumers, which supports U.S. businesses and U.S. jobs" and that it "ignores the value added to the U.S. economy by unauthorized workers, particularly in the service sector."[7]

Americans' Jobs

If FAIR has the tax argument wrong, then are they wrong about undocumented workers taking Americans' jobs? The dirty secret is that illegal immigration is profitable to U.S. employers. Unauthorized immigrants provide manpower in low-end jobs at a time when the number of low-skilled native-born workers is falling. Unauthorized immigrants not only provide cheap labor but also quickly respond to changes in labor markets by moving to other regions or returning to their native countries. The Obama administration points to stepped-up enforcement for the dramatic decline in illegal immigration since 2008, but research shows that the lingering U.S. recession and the shrinking U.S. demand for low-skilled labor are equally important in explaining this decline.[8]

Regardless, most economists believe that few citizens would notice a change in their paychecks if the undocumented suddenly disappeared. That's because few Americans compete with the undocumented. Once a migration stream is established between a sending country, like Mexico, and the United States and new arrivals come to be associated with certain low-skilled jobs, these jobs are labeled *immigrant work,* and few native-born workers will do them. Farm labor, food processing, construction, and service jobs are the most familiar of these jobs.[9] Although poorly educated Americans who work in low-end jobs will see their wages decline by 3 to 8 percent (around $25 per week), remember that the undocumented do not just fill jobs but create jobs through the things they buy and the services they use.[10] Economist Gordon Hanson writes, "Illegal immigration's overall impact on the US economy is small. The small net gain that remains after subtracting US workers' losses from US employers' gains is tiny. If we account for the small fiscal burden that unauthorized immigrants impose, the overall economic benefit is close enough to zero to be essentially a wash."[11]

Arizona's and Alabama's Anti-immigration Laws

So FAIR and similar organizations have gotten it wrong. Immigrants, legal and illegal, pay for the services they use through federal, state, and local taxes. In addition, undocumented workers do jobs that native-born Americans will not. But the studies published by FAIR and other anti-immigration groups hit the national media and help shape public policy. What happens when FAIR and anti-immigrant organizations get their way? What happens when laws are passed that drive the documented and undocumented out of a state? This is precisely what happened in Arizona and Alabama. What has been the impact? Have the purported economic benefits been realized? Have the states experienced any unexpected costs?

Arizona's Support Our Law Enforcement and Safe Neighborhoods Act was one of the first anti–illegal immigration bills passed by a state government. Governor Jan Brewer signed it into law on April 23, 2010, but a federal judge blocked the implementation of its most controversial provisions on constitutional grounds.[12]

The Arizona act makes it a misdemeanor for an alien to be in Arizona without carrying documents, requires law enforcement to determine an individual's immigration status during a "lawful stop," bars state officials from hampering the enforcement of federal immigration laws, and cracks down on sheltering, hiring, and transporting illegal aliens. The law is specifically designed to trigger a mass exodus of undocumented immigrants from the state by making attrition through enforcement the state's immigration policy. Although Arizona's law has not been fully implemented, the Immigration Policy Center has analyzed its potential impact and concluded that "the state's approach would have devastating economic consequences." Deporting the state's estimated 470,000 undocumented residents would reduce employment 17.2 percent, lead to 581,000 lost jobs, shrink the state's economy by $48.8 billion, and slash sales tax revenue by 10.1 percent.[13] The exodus has already begun. The Department of Homeland Security estimates there were 360,000 illegal immigrants in Arizona in January 2011, down 110,000 in a single year.[14]

What would happen, though, if Arizona pursued a proimmigrant policy, one that permitted the undocumented to fully participate in the state's economy? The Immigration Policy Center estimates that employment would increase by 17.2 percent, 261,000 jobs would be created, incomes would rise by $5.6 billion, and tax revenues would climb by $1.68 billion.[15]

Governor Robert J. Bentley signed Alabama's Beason-Hammon Alabama Taxpayer and Citizen Protection Act on June 9, 2011, and like the Arizona law, a federal judge blocked several of its most controversial provisions. The Alabama law, like Arizona's, expands police powers to stop, detain, and arrest illegal immigrants but goes further, prohibiting illegal immigrants from receiving any state benefits, including attending the state's publicly supported colleges and universities. More disturbing, K–12 school officials are required to verify students' immigration status, although the Supreme Court, more than thirty years ago, ruled that these students have a right to attend. In addition, the law prohibits the transporting or harboring of illegal immigrants, landlords from renting property to illegal immigrants, and employers from knowingly hiring illegal immigrants, and it deems contracts entered into by illegal immigrants null and void.[16]

The Center for Business and Economic Research at the University of Alabama performed a cost-benefit analysis on the new legislation. The center identified the following potential benefits of driving out the undocumented: savings from eliminated services; increased safety; and increased business, employment, and educational opportunities for native-born Alabamans. Their analysis identified the costs as follows: implementing, enforcing, and defending the law and inconveniencing citizens, legal residents, and businesses. The center's more serious concern was the loss of the income and spending power of undocumented workers and their families. If the state's 40,000 to 80,000 undocumented workers were to leave, then 70,000 to 140,000 jobs would be lost, Alabama's gross state product would decline by 1.3 to 6.2 percent, state income and sales tax revenue would drop by $56.7 to $264.5 million, and local sales tax collections would shrink by $20 million to $93.1 million.[17]

Alabama is already reeling from the effects of the law. The state had a public relations fiasco in 2011 when, in a span of a few days, the state police used the new law to arrest the German director of the state's Mercedes-Benz plant and a Japanese executive at a nearby Honda plant.[18] The *St. Louis Post-Dispatch* reveled in Alabama's embarrassment by publishing an open letter to foreign car companies encouraging them to pack their bags and move to the rival car-producing state of Missouri. The legislator who introduced the bill squirmed under the media spotlight. The Mercedes-Benz plant in Tuscaloosa is vital to the state's economy, as is Honda's $1.4 billion plant in Lincoln, which employs 4,000 workers.

The effects of the new law are being felt not just in Tuscaloosa and Lincoln but statewide. A serious labor shortage spread across the state's important agricultural sector after Hispanic pickers fled the state.[19] No-shows of whole crews have heavily hit the construction industry.[20] Tuscaloosa contractor Bob McNelly reports, "Hispanics, documented and undocumented, dominate anything to do with masonry, concrete, framing, roofing, and landscaping. There are very few subcontractors I work with that don't have a Hispanic workforce." He adds, "It's not the pay rate. It's the fact that they work harder than anyone. It's the work ethic."[21] A November 20, 2011, editorial in the *Tuscaloosa News* weighs in that the "immigration law is becoming the greatest threat to the state's economy and job creation." The editorial urges Republican lawmakers, who have said they are considering revisions to the law, to scrap it altogether.[22]

Maybe the legislature should have carefully read the University of Alabama researcher's concluding passage in the analysis: "While the law's costs are certain and some are large, it is not clear that the benefits will be realized. From an economist's perspective, the question Alabama and its legislature have to ponder is this: Are the benefits of the new immigration law worth the costs?"[23] And like Arizona, there is evidence that the policy is working to drive the undocumented out of the state. The state's agricultural and construction industries are reporting serious labor shortages. More disturbing are reports of Hispanic students vanishing from Alabama schools after the immigration law's passage.

These are state laws. What happens when a community takes immigration control into its own hands? This was precisely what Riverside, New Jersey, did, much to its regret. Riverside is a small working-class town of 8,000 across the Delaware River from Philadelphia. In the 2000s the region's building boom drew 5,000 new residents to the town, most of them undocumented Brazilians. The town responded by passing the Riverside Township Illegal Immigration Relief Act, which was designed to impose heavy fines and jail sentences on and revoke the business licenses of employers who hired undocumented immigrants and of landlords who rented to them. Though the ordinance was never enforced, 75 percent of Riverside's immigrant population fled, resulting in nearly half of the town's businesses closing. Riverside's downtown revitalization ended when immigrant buying power evaporated and the loss of tax revenue, along with the legal fees spent defending the ordinance, forced the town to slash services. More important, the economic growth that had benefited all residents was lost.[24]

On June 25, 2012, the Supreme Court announced its ruling in

Arizona v. United States, a lawsuit brought against Arizona by the Obama administration. The ruling cast a shadow on the constitutionality of similar laws in Alabama, Georgia, and Florida, as well as ordinances like Riverside's. The high court struck down provisions of Arizona's law that required all immigrants to carry immigration papers, made it a violation of Arizona law for an undocumented immigrant to seek or hold a job, and allowed police to arrest suspected undocumented immigrants without warrants. The court upheld, however, a key provision that allowed state and local police to check the immigration status of people they stopped or detained if a "reasonable suspicion" existed that they were in the country illegally. The court left open the possibility for challenges to the remaining provision of the law if it led to racial and ethnic profiling. The bottom line was that the majority ruled Arizona had usurped federal authority in the area of immigration enforcement and reaffirmed the role of the federal government in immigration law and its enforcement.[25]

Contributions to the Economy

FAIR and other anti-immigrant organizations also argue that documented and undocumented immigrants have little impact on our economy, which is far from the truth. The Selig Center for Economic Growth is the public service unit of the University of Georgia's Terry College of Business. It is nationally known for its economic impact and outlook studies. In 2011 the center reported that the nation's total buying power had risen from $7.3 to $11.1 trillion in the past decade, and they forecasted that it would rise to $14.1 trillion by 2015. The center predicted that Hispanics and Asians would significantly contribute to this growth.[26]

The center's director and the author of the report, Jeff Humphreys, writes, "Minorities have a lot of economic clout, and these groups in particular are experiencing growth in buying power that greatly exceeds that of the general population." He goes on to note that "the Hispanic market alone, at $1 trillion, is larger than the entire economies of all but 14 countries in the world." More important, Hispanic buying power is expected to grow 50 percent by 2015 to $1.5 trillion. The rate of growth in Hispanic buying power tops that of all other racial and ethnic groups, as well as the rate of growth of the nation's overall buying power. To account for this growth, Humphreys points to rising educational levels, growing middle-income employment, increased entrepreneurial activity, and the group's upward social mobility. The picture for Asians is even rosier. As a group, Asians are more highly educated than the average American and are often employed in management and the professions, and their buying power is expected to grow from $544 billion in 2010 to $775 billion in 2015, a 42 percent increase.

Though most Asians and Hispanics live in traditional gateway states like California, Arizona, New Mexico, New York, and Texas, other states are experiencing significant economic growth in minority buying power. For example, the top-ten states in the growth of Hispanic buying power over the past decade are South Dakota (253 percent), North Dakota (237 percent), Arkansas (229 percent), Alabama (228 percent), South Carolina (226 percent), Maine (222 percent), Tennessee (220 percent), West Virginia (211 percent), Mississippi (206 percent), and Maryland (204 percent).[27] As the baby boom generation reaches retirement, the buying power and tax receipts of minorities will become increasingly important in state economies. Arkansas is a good example. The 2010 purchasing power of Arkansas's Hispanics totaled $3.3 billion—an increase of 1,908.2 percent since 1990. Asian buying power totaled $1.1 billion—an increase of 656.1 percent since 1990. Arkansas's 5,436 Hispanic-owned businesses had sales and receipts of $821 million and employed 4,269 people in 2007 (the last year for which data are available). In addition, the state's 3,322 Asian-owned businesses had sales and receipts of $855.7 million and employed 7,285 people in 2007. If all unauthorized immigrants left Arkansas, the state would lose $798 million in economic activity, $354 million in gross state product, and approximately 6,600 jobs.[28]

Once again, the anti-immigration groups have it wrong. Economic data consistently show the vital role minorities play in the nation's economy. Today, Hispanics and Asians provide nearly 14 percent of the nation's total purchasing power, and in 2010, Hispanic and Asian businesses racked up sales of $857 billion and employed 4.7 million workers. This economic activity is vital to the nation, our states, and our communities.

Economic Reasons for the DREAM Act

On this point I have explored claims made by FAIR and other anti-immigration groups and their attacks on immigration reform in general and the DREAM Act in particular. I explore these issues in more depth in Chapter 6, but let me here share some compelling economic reasons for the passage of the DREAM Act.

First, giving undocumented students access to affordable higher education and legal employment would mean better jobs, higher incomes, and an expanding tax base. It would keep our best and brightest in our states and contribute to the human capital of our nation. It would mean buying homes, opening businesses, investing, and expanding the buying power of all Americans. A 2010 study by UCLA's North American Integration and Development Center estimates that passage of the DREAM Act would increase the total earnings of DREAM Act beneficiaries by $1.4 trillion to $3.6 trillion over the course of their working lives.[29]

Second, taxpayers would save money because more undocumented students would stay in school. Giving young people hope for college, legal employment, citizenship, and a better and more secure life would reduce social service and health costs.

Third, passing the act would help our universities. In a few short years, the millennial generation will be out of college, and our universities will have idle capacity. Nationally, there are only 65,000 undocumented high school graduates each year—a miniscule number in comparison with the 20.5 million college students in the United States. The DREAM Act would allow universities to tap this idle capacity and create an additional income stream.

Finally, it would be good for our national defense. Over the next thirty years, the majority of Americans will be from minority groups—African American, Hispanic, and Asian. Eight percent of our military are currently foreign-born. The DREAM Act would provide a path to citizenship for the undocumented who serve honorably and address the recruiting shortage that looms in the future.

As I have demonstrated, most economists and labor-market experts believe FAIR has gotten the economic argument wrong. Studies consistently show that immigrants grow the economy, expand the demand for goods and services, and create jobs. They pay taxes at the federal, state, and local levels and make contributions to Social Security, Medicare, and unemployment insurance programs, from which they receive no benefits. In addition, studies like the one published by the nonpartisan Congressional Budget Office find that undocumented immigrants contribute more in taxes than they cost in social services.

We are a nation created by four waves of immigration, and throughout our history we have used the skills, talents, and entrepreneurial spirits of our newest residents to grow our economy and raise the fortunes of all Americans. This process has made America the envy of the world, and by looking at our history, we can know that the DREAM Act makes sense, because it would benefit us all.

FOUR

Salsa, America's Number-One Condiment

Culture. They are changing our national character. We are a white, Christian nation grounded in a European heritage.

I n 2010 the United States granted permanent legal residency to 1.1 million immigrants—Germans, Greeks, Swedes, Norwegians, Japanese, Koreans, Chinese, Laotians, Vietnamese, Ethiopians, Columbians, Nigerians, Kenyans, French, English, Irish, Russians, Italians, Croatians, Peruvians, Poles, Czechs, Hungarians, Cubans, Mexicans, Salvadorans, Nicaraguans, and people of more than two hundred other nationalities.[1] Now, as in our past, no nation in history has accepted as its citizens, albeit sometimes reluctantly, more people from more backgrounds than has the United States. On the one hand, it is one of our nation's strengths; we have brought together the talents and the perspectives of many cultures in defining our national character. On the other hand, immigration has been a source of great division, at times creating cleavages that weakened our political and social fabric. The miracle that is America is that such a diverse collection of peoples can live together in peace.

The twentieth century witnessed the transformation of the United States from a predominately white population rooted in Western culture to a society with a rich array of racial, ethnic, and religious minorities. At the beginning of the twentieth century, the U.S. population was 87 percent white. The nonwhite minority was primarily composed of African Americans living in the rural South. At the beginning of the twenty-first century, whites still accounted for 72 percent of the U.S. population, but a profound demographic shift is under way. In May

2012, the Census Bureau reported that, for the first time in our history, more minority children (African American, Hispanic, and Asian) than white children were born here.[2] Few Americans realize that by the end of the next decade, the majority of our children will be from minority groups, and by the end of the following decade, the majority of Americans will be from these minority groups. In the next thirty years, the United States will become significantly more racially and ethnically diverse than it is today.[3]

We have a long history of immigration, and our past shows that we have grown and prospered by it. At the beginning of the twentieth century, many Americans were concerned about the growing number of immigrants from eastern, central, and southern Europe, and industrialization and urbanization were the forces transforming our nation and its economy. At the beginning of this century, immigration again is a concern of Americans, but this time the immigrants are from Latin America and Asia and globalization is transforming the nation and its economy.[4]

Although our society was created out of successive waves of migration, Americans are divided in their beliefs about the long-term effects of this growing diversity. Like so much in our political discourse, the groups on the extremes have defined the immigration debate. FAIR, for example, has as its goals "to end illegal immigration through enforcement of existing immigration laws" and "to set legal immigration at the lowest feasible levels consistent with the national security, economic, demographic, environmental and socio-cultural interests." They also advocate the "[end] of mass immigration to the United States as a solution to international problems" and the end of the immigration that undermines "opportunities for America's poor and vulnerable citizens." FAIR supports a temporary moratorium on all immigration to allow a national debate and the passage of comprehensive immigration reform and a return to "more traditional [immigration] levels of about 300,000 a year."[5] On the other side are groups like the Cato Institute, a limited government and free-market think tank. They advocate open immigration, believing it strengthens and enriches American culture, expands and diversifies our labor market, increases the total output of the economy, and raises the standard of living of American citizens.[6]

Googling *immigration* with *pro, anti, legal,* and *illegal,* I found thou-

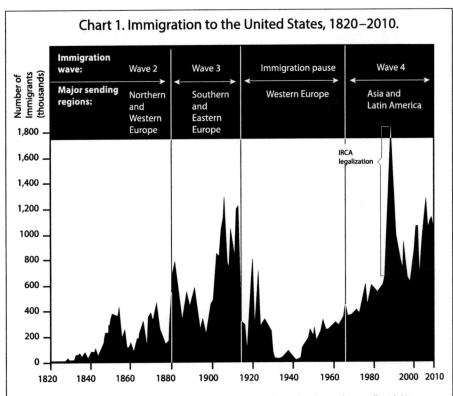

Chart 1. Immigration to the United States, 1820–2010.

Immigration wave:	Wave 2	Wave 3	Immigration pause	Wave 4
Major sending regions:	Northern and Western Europe	Southern and Eastern Europe	Western Europe	Asia and Latin America

IRCA legalization

Note: Wave 1 (not shown here) includes the period from initial European settlement through 1820. Almost 4 million inhabitants were counted in the 1790 census (the nation's first), including 700,000 slaves. By 1820 the nation's population grew to 9.6 million, including 1.5 million slaves. The English made up 60 percent of the population in this wave, but there were also Scots, Irish, Germans, and other northern Europeans. Most of the slave trade was centered in West Africa. The 1820 census collected immigration data for the first time.

"IRC legalization" refers to the amnesty provisions of the Immigration Reform and Control Act of 1986— approximately 2.7 million undocumented residents obtained legal status.

Sources: U.S. Census Bureau, "Census of Population and Housing," U.S. Census Bureau website, http://www.census.gov/prod/www/abs/decennial; Department of Homeland Security, "2011 Yearbook of Immigration Statistics," Table 1, Department of Homeland Security website, http://www.dhs.gov/sites/default/files/publications/immigration-statistics/yearbook/2011/ois_yb_2011.pdf.

sands of advocacy groups across the country. Pro-immigration groups include We Are America Alliance, Border Angels, American Immigration Lawyers Association, and New American Opportunity Campaign. We Are America Alliance, for example, consists of community, labor, and religious organizations that lobby Congress for amnesty for the nation's undocumented.

Anti-immigration groups also abound. They include the American Immigration Control Foundation, the National Organization for European American Rights (NOFEAR), NumbersUSA, and Project USA.

One of the most active is the Minutemen. The group made head-lines by organizing their own volunteer force to patrol sections of the U.S.–Mexico border. The Minutemen like to refer to themselves as the "local neighborhood watch" of the border.[7]

But most groups are in the middle, with narrowly defined goals. Typical are think tanks like the American Immigration Council, concerned with protecting the rights of foreigners in the United States, and the Migration Policy Institute, a nonpartisan, nonprofit think tank that analyzes the movement of people worldwide. Also in the middle are ethnic-based groups like the Japanese-American Citizens League, who favor more immigration from their country and region.

Are the critics of immigration correct? Is our newest wave of immigration fundamentally changing our society? Will the new-est wave of immigrants overwhelm traditional American culture? If left unchecked, will the newest immigrants wipe away our European, Christian heritage? Should we be concerned? Should we pursue drastic measures to stem the tide?

Opposition to immigration, or nativism, is common in countries with histories of mass immigration such as Australia, Canada, New Zealand, and the United States. In recent years a nativist movement has been growing in Europe in response to increased immigration from eastern Europe, Africa, and the Middle East. Regardless of the country, common themes among the opposition are fears that the immigrants will change and despoil existing cultural values and that immigrant hos-tility to their new culture means they can never be assimilated.[8]

We have a long anti-immigration tradition in the United States stretching back to the earliest days of the republic. Benjamin Franklin and Thomas Jefferson shared an antipathy for Germans. President John Adams in 1798 signed the Alien and Sedition Act, which limited the full political participation of some immigrants. In subsequent generations nativists have focused on Catholics, Jews, Germans, and Chinese, and today, the targets are Latinos and Asians. Therefore, it is not surprising that nativists would be alarmed by the size and national origins of the fourth wave of immigration and the reality that the nation will be sig-nificantly more racially and ethnically diverse in the next generation. But their fears and beliefs are based on a false assumption: that the cul-ture and traditions of our newest immigrants will displace our current ones. All one needs to do is look at our economic and social history to see that the nativist position is not true.[9]

Fifty years of demographic research shows that immigrants pulled to this nation for its economic opportunities differ from the neighbors they left behind. Immigrants who are pulled here for economic opportunities tend to be better educated, more entrepreneurial, harder-working, and in their prime working years. In addition, they pass on these values to their children. There is evidence that they strengthen and enrich American culture, increase the total output of the economy, and raise the standard of living of all Americans. And plenty of evidence supports these statements.[10] New businesses are the single-best creators of new jobs, and even with current visa barriers, in 2010 immigrants were more than twice as likely as native-born Americans to start a business. During the high-tech boom, immigrants founded or cofounded 25 percent of all high-tech companies, creating 450,000 jobs. Forty-five percent of Fortune 500 companies were founded by immigrants or their children. So now, as in our past, immigration is a vital part of a dynamic, growing economy.[11]

The same is true of culture. Anti-immigration groups would lead us to believe that the fourth wave of immigration will overwhelm American culture and make it fundamentally different, that somehow more than two centuries of European heritage will be wiped away in a generation or two, and that American culture, not the immigrants' culture, will change. But history and experience teach us that we can trust the foundations of our culture and institutions. To even discuss immigration, we must assume assimilation. When an immigrant group enters an existing society, the new members must fit into the social structure, and central to this process is the charter group, the socially, politically, and economically powerful of the host society, who determine, first, who gets in and, second, what opportunities they will have in the society. The familiar acronym WASP (White Anglo-Saxon Protestant) describes the charter group for most of our history, and there is no better example of their power and influence than our immigration laws. For example, Congress passed the Chinese Exclusion Act in 1882, which specifically limited Chinese immigration in response to nativists on the West Coast. Forty years later, Congress passed the Immigration Act of 1924, which limited immigration through a strict quota system, with the result that people from only northern European countries, with cultures similar to that of the charter group, were likely to get in. Similar motivations have shaped our current laws. Throughout our history Congress has enacted these laws under pressure from interest groups demanding that the federal government reduce immigration to protect American culture. Often, the demands have happened to coincide with the interests or anxieties of the charter group.[12]

WASPs are descendants of the western and northern Europeans who arrived on our shores during our first and second waves of immigration in the seventeenth, eighteenth, and nineteenth centuries. Because they controlled and, in many respects, continue to control the key institutions of our society, they form the social framework to which the immigrant group must adapt. If the immigrant group is similar to the charter group, then the process will be relatively smooth and rapid. If major differences exist, then the process will be slow and erratic.

It is a two-step process. In the first step immigrants acquire the behaviors, attitudes, sentiments, values, language, and history of American society. The process has worked when they speak English and think of themselves as Americans. In the second step ethnic groups move out of low-paying, unskilled jobs into key decision-making positions in government, business, and other spheres of society. When successful, in but a few generations the new group is absorbed into American society, and the group is reminded of its ethnic ancestry only by its surnames and family traditions. This is the so-called melting pot model, and although several competing theories exist, they all recognize that assimilation takes time and that the rate of assimilation varies by ethnic group. For example, although African Americans successfully assimilated behaviors of American society centuries ago, only recently have blacks completed the entire two-step process of assimilation and begun to assume key positions in society, such as corporate leaders and president of the United States. And members of my generation can remember the election of President John F. Kennedy, an event that many Americans feel marks the final stage of assimilation of Irish Americans. The elections of governors Bobby Jindal (LA) and Nikki Haley (SC), who are second-generation Indians, and Senator

Marco Rubio, a second-generation Cuban, suggest that the process is well under way for our latest immigration wave.[13]

The absurdity of the anti-immigration arguments is found in our history. More Americans trace their ancestry to Germany (15.2 percent) than to any other country. Is German our national language? Is Catholicism our state religion? We have created a pluralistic society by selectively absorbing culture from each immigrant wave and thereby enriching American culture. Obvious examples of this selection process include food and drink, like pilsner beer, a brewing style borrowed from Germans that dominates our beer market; pizza, which has become the nation's favorite food; and salsa, which has replaced catsup as the nation's number-one condiment. Less visible but equally important are nonmaterial cultural items that have entered into the English we speak, the music we enjoy, and the styles we wear. But there is another side of the assimilation process—our society's powerful norming, which fosters the learning of English and the adopting of core American values. If the anti-immigration groups were correct, then the 40 million immigrants in the third wave would have created deep social cleavages, eroding our common values and weakening the social glue that holds us together. And if these things had occurred, we would be able to pick up this shift through public opinion polling and social science research.

The United States is the most diverse, multicultural, and multiethnic nation on earth. Thousands of groups that differ on political and social ideologies, religion, race, and ethnicity live here, but there is strong evidence that we, now as in the past, are united by core democratic values that are expressed in our Declaration of Independence and Constitution. They are life, liberty, and the pursuit of happiness and a commitment to the common good, justice, equality, diversity, truth, popular sovereignty, and patriotism. We learn them in our civics and history classes; we reaffirm them when we are threatened by events like 9/11; we celebrate them on the Fourth of July; we recognize those who have sacrificed for them on Veterans Day; and we demand that immigrants learn them before they become naturalized U.S. citizens.

Since the 1960s, social scientists have been asking Americans about their core values.[14] We have fifty years of data, and if the critics were right—that indeed the fourth wave was threatening our culture and our way of life—then this threat would be reflected as a shift in our value system.

Wayne Baker, a researcher at the University of Michigan's Institute for Social Research, explores this question of values in *Americans' Evolving Values Surveys in 2009–2010*.[15] Rather than finding a shift in core values and a decline in our commitments to them, he discovered the opposite. Many values, like liberty, the pursuit of happiness, justice, equality, and democracy, have been remarkably stable over generations and are consistent with the ideological principles described by Thomas Jefferson more than two hundred years ago. The following are the eight core values that Baker found most Americans share:

> *Patriotism.* The vast majority of Americans have a deep emotional commitment to this nation, and even if they oppose a government policy, they do it with the belief that it will make their society better.
>
> *Belief in God.* Two-thirds of Americans believe in God, the highest percentage of any nation in the developed world.
>
> *Self-reliance.* Individualism, autonomy, liberty, and sovereignty are ideals that can be traced back to the works of Thomas Jefferson and are still deeply held by the vast majority of Americans. Nearly 90 percent of Americans say they would rather depend on themselves than others.
>
> *Achievement and success.* Seventy-five percent of Americans agree that getting ahead is important to them. Although recognizing that forces beyond one's control, like a recession, can affect life chances, the vast majority believes that getting ahead is the result of an individual's talents, skills, education, and hard work.
>
> *Equal opportunities.* Over 90 percent of Americans agree that everyone should have equal opportunities, although there is less agreement over the idea of equality of outcomes.
>
> *Freedom and liberty.* This value is one of the most deeply held by Americans and a sign of a vibrant democracy.
>
> *Respect.* More than 90 percent of Americans agree that respect for people of different racial, ethnic, and religious groups is important

to them. More than 70 percent of Americans say that immigrants should adopt American values.

Free market. Even during these perilous economic times, nearly three-quarters of Americans agree that a free market is the best way to run our economy. A commitment to free markets is intertwined with other core values, like freedom, liberty, individualism, achievement, and equality.

Research shows that today, as in our past, Americans share a broad consensus on the core values that shape this society. Moreover, the values have been remarkably resilient across generations and have been adopted by our four waves of immigrants. Immigrant groups, rather than being alien and hostile to our culture and society, have been assimilated into the American social framework. Why would it be otherwise? They have come to the United States for freedom and economic opportunities. They yearn to be a part of American society.

I began researching northwest Arkansas's Hispanic community in 2007, and most of my interviews and focus groups revolved around issues of assimilation. In 2011, I focused my research on undocumented children and young adults. Like undocumented youth nationwide, my subjects were brought to the United States at a very young age, attended our public schools, often lived in predominantly white neighborhoods, spoke American-accented English, and were Americans in every way, except their immigration status. They had been socialized as Americans in our schools, neighborhoods, and communities. I asked these students several questions in order to determine their values—for example, "What would you like the readers of this book to know about you?" and, "What would you want them to know about the DREAM Act?" Their responses did not reveal them to be members of an alien, hostile culture or a group that could never be assimilated. I found quite the opposite, in fact—that they had already been assimilated. In the following interviews, these DREAMers express many of Baker's core American values.

Mirna is in her twenties, lives in the Kansas City area, and has been a DREAMer since her teens. She was educated in public schools, speaks unaccented English, and has been arrested for her political activism. She recently came out and declared she was undocumented and unafraid. The following are Mirna's answers to my questions:

You know how many people say I can tell who's undocumented and who's not—you can't. I might have been your neighbor. I might have competed with you. I might have helped you: I'm a volunteer. I'm an asset, not a burden. I pay taxes. I have my own business. There's no harm I mean to the country but to make it better. . . . I want you to know that I am American, that I am patriotic, that I love this country, that I would die for this country. My only intention is to make it better in every single way.

I'm not a hardcore—I know a lot of people associate DREAMers and social activists with liberalists who want to see no government and things like that. I am religious. I have moral values. I grew up conservative. My only hope is to be able to stay in a country that I call home, with my family. And live freely. Not in the golden cage. I want to be able to serve and do that without any restrictions.

Mirna's statement reflects the core values of patriotism, belief in God, self-reliance, achievement and success, and free markets. And to her the DREAM Act incorporates the core American values of equal opportunities, freedom, liberty, and respect.

Jazmin was five when her mother brought her to the United States from Mexico to escape an abusive husband. Her mother and siblings shared a small trailer with another family for several years until her mother could find work. Jazmin is the product of a small, rural school district, and even though she did not have certified teachers in math and natural science, she excelled academically and received a privately funded scholarship to the University of Arkansas. Graduating with honors in a natural science, she is the poster child for the American Dream, a person of modest background who has succeeded in one of the most difficult majors on any campus. Though Jazmin's words express her pain over opportunities denied and talents ignored and devalued, they also show the underlying values that guide her: achievement and success, self-reliance, equal opportunities, and respect:

I've always had the outlook that you have to work hard for whatever you want. That things shouldn't just be given to you. That even if you're intelligent and that you have the capability of doing really well in a school or a job, you should still have something to back it up. I just sort of want the chance to prove myself.

And every single time I've read articles in the *Traveler* of where people just sort of blanket call undocumented students—the un-documented students who are getting private scholarships that Chancellor Gearhart worked out to pay our out-of-state tuition difference—calling us criminals. And I don't feel like a criminal. I don't feel that what I'm doing is criminal in any way. . . . I don't want everything to be handed for me. I don't want someone to just give me citizenship tomorrow. I mean, I would be willing to just work for it and show everyone that I'm, that I'm respon-sible enough that you can trust me with legal status here in this country.

Jazmin repeatedly returns to the issue of equal opportunity and oppor-tunities based on merit in her interview. She was one of the top stu-dents in her field in the United States and was repeatedly passed over for research and other opportunities because of her undocumented status.

Just because she had this nine-digit number attached to her was so frustrating to me, and it made me feel that what I was capable of wasn't what everyone else sees. That when it comes down to it, if you don't have this number attached to your name that you are . . . you are less than everyone else.

Ricardo, a twenty-eight-year-old Texas resident, became the first person in his family to earn a college degree, a degree made possible by Texas's DREAM Act, which provided not only in-state tuition but state-funded financial aid. His words mirror the values of patriotism, self-reliance, achievement and success, and equal opportunities:

Whatever you want in life, you have to work for it. If someone else is trying to compete with you, you work extra hard and put your energy into it. The message is, we're not the competition here. We're not the enemy here. We're here to make this coun-try great. We're here to contribute.

In rereading these interviews, I was again struck by the feeling that we are doing something wrong. These are remarkable young people, bright, intelligent, and ambitious, asking only for the chance to succeed in the only society they know, to pursue the American Dream.

Critics of immigration and the DREAM Act frame their arguments in terms of loss—the loss of American culture, the loss of employment and economic opportunities for U.S. citizens, and the loss of national security. I look at it differently. These young people are an invaluable economic and cultural asset that we cannot afford to squander. The twentieth century is often called the American Century. During this century we found our national character and became a superpower. Much has changed in the first decade of the twenty-first century, and global economic competition has replaced the competition between two superpowers. Only the education, skills, and talents of our people and their contributions to the global economy will make the twenty-first century an American Century, too. In *Deciphering the City* I describe the following qualities of this nation that I believe will make America succeed:

- We are blessed with geography. We are on the Pacific and the Atlantic Rims, with economic and cultural ties to the vibrant economies of both Asia and Europe.
- We are blessed with an ethnically, racially, and religiously diverse society that has links to most of the nations in the world. Although multicultural, multiethnic, and multilingual, we are bound together by a single language—English—the language of world commerce. We openly accept immigrants and their talents and money. We protect their constitutional rights, and we embrace them as citizens.
- We have the most diverse, innovative, and efficient capital markets in the world.
- We have an honest legal and regulatory environment, and our government, financial institutions, and corporations are the most transparent in the world. We have a legal right to government and financial information.
- We have a system of bankruptcy laws that encourages people to take risks and, if they fail, to try again.
- We have a relatively fluid stratification system. We are becoming a society based on merit.
- We have a decentralized decision-making process in our federal system that is capable of changing to meet the needs of our society in the twenty-first century.
- We have an open and mobile workforce.

- We accept the innovator, the oddball, and the maverick.
- Our corporations have already gone through downsizing, privatizing, networking, deregulation, re-engineering, streamlining, and restructuring in order to exploit the democratization of finance, technology, information, and decision-making. These corporations excel in a fast-moving, networked global economy.
- We have a system of deeply rooted entrepreneurship and a tax system that allows the risk-taker to keep what he or she earns.
- We have environmentally protected open spaces and small towns.
- We have the largest and best system of higher education in the world.
- Finally and most important, we have the world's largest pool of symbolic analysts—problem identifiers, problem solvers, and innovators who can visualize new uses of existing technologies. We have the richest and most diverse innovation clusters in the world where our symbolic analysts live, work, and learn from one another.

In short, we have a society designed for the global economy in the twenty-first century, and the talents, skills, and entrepreneurial spirits of the DREAMers and other immigrants are important contributors to this society.

Final Thoughts

There are four main characteristics of the fourth wave of immigration to the United States. First, in 2010, 36.7 million (12 percent) of the population were foreign-born, and another 33 million (11 percent) were native-born with at least one foreign-born parent, making one in five people either first- or second-generation U.S. residents.

Second, there are 11.2 million unauthorized immigrants in the United States. The number has declined and stabilized from its high of 12 million in 2008.

Third, documented and undocumented immigrant labor is indispensable to the agriculture, service, and construction sectors of the U.S. economy. Increasingly, highly educated and skilled immigrants are playing a critical role in the information- and knowledge-based sectors of our economy. Immigrants are twice as likely as native-born Americans to open new businesses, and 45 percent of Fortune 500 companies were founded by immigrants or the children of immigrants.

Fourth, the size of the nation's fourth wave of immigration has created a demographic echo. More than 70 million people in the United States are immigrants or the children of immigrants, and as a result the majority of American children will be of Hispanic, Asian, or African American heritage by the next decade. Most of the growth in the next generation will be through immigration or children born to immigrants. Never before in our history have immigrants made up so large a share of the youngest Americans, and undocumented children and young adults are an important part of this group.

The current political debate over undocumented immigrants in the United States has largely ignored the plight of undocumented children. There are approximately 2.1 million undocumented children and young adults in the United States, 15 percent of the undocumented immigrants now living in this country. Their parents brought them here illegally. They have been socialized in our schools and neighborhoods as Americans. They have few or no ties with kin from or memories of their countries of their origin. Most do not fluently speak their parents' language, and even fewer can read or write it. A 1982 ruling by the Supreme Court requires school districts to provide primary and secondary educations to the undocumented but does not extend post-secondary education benefits like in-state tuition to the undocumented. With no path to citizenship, only a fraction of undocumented high school graduates go to college. Even if they graduate, they cannot work here legally. Always hanging over their heads is the specter of deportation to a country they do not know and have neither the network nor the skills to navigate. The bottom line is that we are wasting our nation's investment in these children, and this wasted talent imposes financial and emotional costs on these youth and social and economic costs on all of us.

Therefore, the passage of comprehensive immigration reform and a federal DREAM Act makes demographic and economic sense. The accelerating growth of this nation's minority youth heralds an increasingly diverse child population and labor force. No doubt, it poses challenges to our education, social, economic, and political institutions, but preparing minority and immigrant children for full participation in our society gives us distinct economic advantages. Many Asian and European nations have a declining birth rate and an aging labor force. By 2030 the United States will have a younger workforce than China, Japan, Korea, and most of Europe. With the rapidly aging white population, our nation will depend on the skills and educations of our emerging majority of minorities for the skills of our labor force and the vitality of our economy. Clearly, the future of these youth as they seek to integrate socially and economically into this society is of vital interest to all Americans, and education is central to this process.

FIVE

The Melting Pot, Mixed with Just a Few New Ingredients

Assimilation. Undocumented immigrants will not be a part of the melting pot, because they live in insular, non-English-speaking communities bound by networks of kin and friends.

We are a nation shaped by four waves of immigrants, the last two having the greatest impact, because of their size and diversity. During the third wave, which began in the 1860s and ended in the 1920s, the nation absorbed 24 million immigrants from eastern and southern Europe, reaching a peak of 15 percent of the population in 1890, the largest percentage in our history. The arrival of the Great Depression and the enactment of anti-immigration laws in the 1920s shut down the third wave, and the volume of immigration did not recover until the 1970s. Since the 1970s, however, the United States has accepted more than 40 million immigrants, reaching a peak of 13 percent of the population in 2010, and the source of this immigration has shifted again, this time from Europe to Latin America and Asia. Today, as with the generations before us, many Americans are struggling to understand not only the impact of immigration on our society but also the culture and experiences of the current wave of immigrants.

History is repeating itself. Although separated by a century, the two waves of immigrants have many things in common. The immigrants in both waves differed from the native-born society in race, dress, customs, language, and religion. Their arrival unleashed vocal anti-immigration groups who successfully framed them as alien and threatening to American culture. In the 1920s groups like the Ku Klux Klan seized on Americans' fears of immigrants and anything un-American;

today, the same role is played by groups like the American Immigrant Control Foundation, the National Organization for European Rights, and the Council of Conservative Citizens. Then, as now, the same arguments are used to keep immigrants out: they are so *different* from us; they can *never* be assimilated, nor do they *want* to be. These early campaigns worked, providing justification for Congress to pass sweeping immigration laws to keep *them* out.

Social scientists use an array of terms—*assimilation, acculturation, integration,* and *incorporation*—to describe the process by which a group entering a host society is eventually absorbed into it. I use *assimilation,* but regardless of the term, all social scientists recognize that the process is a temporal one played out over generations, that the characteristics of both the immigrant group and the host society influence the rate and completeness of the process, and that it is a two-way process: the immigrant group is absorbed, but aspects of its culture persist until absorbed into American culture.

These are the concerns of the host society, but for immigrants the choice is stark and simple. If they want to be accepted as citizens, then they must learn the host society's language and culture and show undivided loyalty to their adopted nation. If they hold on to their culture, keep close ties with their native country, and remain different, then they will not be accepted as citizens nor treated equally. Look to Germany's Turks and France's North Africans for examples of ethnic groups who are not being assimilated. Each choice has costs, and immigrants must decide which is better for them.

The thinking behind assimilation is straightforward. Society cannot be cohesive and stable unless there is a shared culture—language, customs, practices, attitudes, and history—to hold it together. Culture is the blueprint for living, and without shared values, beliefs, and norms, the future of a society would be in question.

Assimilation well describes the experiences of our mostly European third wave, which arrived at the turn of the twentieth century. The question is whether these models will describe the experiences of our current wave. Is our newest wave of immigrants becoming part of our melting pot tradition? Are they being absorbed into our society? Are they on the path to fully participating in our social and political institutions? Are the roles of ethnic neighborhoods and enclaves different for the current wave?

Will our newest immigrants ever fully assimilate? If so, how long will it take? The DREAMers are unique because they are not a true second generation. They were not born here but were brought at a young age and socialized in American schools and communities. Some social scientists wonder if traditional assimilation models can be used to describe the experiences of the 1.5 generation.

American social scientists have been studying the immigrant experience for more than a century, and they use the following four benchmarks to measure a group's assimilation: (1) residential integration, (2) socioeconomic integration, (3) language attainment, and (4) intermarriage. Using these four dimensions of assessment, sociologists have determined that third-wave ethnic groups have been largely absorbed and that their languages, foods, and tastes have been Americanized. The current wave of immigration has arrived so recently that research on their experiences is only now being published. Let's take a look at what researchers have found.

Residential Integration

What is the second-largest Polish city in the world? Chicago. One of the world's largest Armenian cities? Buffalo. What is the most ethnically diverse place on the globe? New York City, where eight hundred languages are spoken and over two hundred countries are represented. What is one of the largest Spanish-speaking cities in the world? Los Angeles. The experiences of Chicago, Buffalo, New York, and Los Angeles are not unique. Exploring the Internet, I found ethnic neighborhoods in almost every large U.S. city, with names like Chinatown, Little Havana, Little Italy, Little India, Little Saigon, Little Pakistan, Ironbound (Portuguese and Brazilian), Germantown, German Village, Dutchtown, Greektown, Irishtown, Japantown, and the ubiquitous Barrio. The name of each reflects the people who live or have lived there, and every major ethnic group who has entered this society is represented in this mosaic of social worlds.

Social scientists know that as long as there have been cities people with similar languages, races, ethnicities, and religions have lived together. The history of our immigrant gateway cities like New York, Boston, Philadelphia, Chicago, Cleveland, Toledo, Pittsburgh,

Figure 1. Immigration to the United States, by Region of Origin, 1970 and 2010

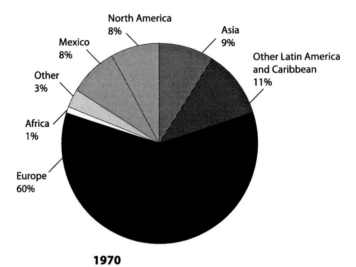

North America
8%

Asia
9%

Mexico
8%

Other Latin America
and Caribbean
11%

Other
3%

Africa
1%

Europe
60%

1970

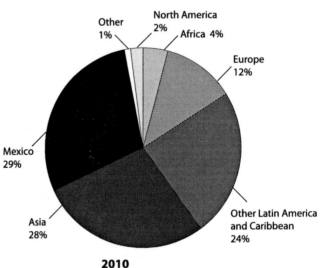

Other
1%

North America
2%

Africa 4%

Europe
12%

Mexico
29%

Other Latin America
and Caribbean
24%

Asia
28%

2010

Sources: Adapted from Michael Jones-Correa, *Contested Ground: Immigration in the United States* (Washington, D.C.: Migration Policy Institute, Transatlantic Council on Migration, 2012). This figure is based on the following sources of data: MPI Data Hub, "Ten Source Countries with the Largest Populations in the United States as Percentages of the Total Foreign-Born Population: 1970," Migration Policy Institute website, http://www.migrationinformation.org/datahub/charts/10.70.shtml; MPI Data Hub, "Ten Source Countries with the Largest Populations in the United States as Percentages of the Total Foreign-Born Population: 2010," Migration Policy Institute website, www.migrationinformation.org/datahub/charts/10.2010.shtml.

Cincinnati, New Orleans, Los Angeles, and San Francisco are filled with examples of ethnic neighborhoods with their own stores, churches, schools, hospitals, social clubs, newspapers, and benevolent societies. The reason they exist is simple. To the recent immigrant the ethnic neighborhood is familiar and safe—a sanctuary that provides a buffer from an alien, strange, and often hostile host society. Immigrants can speak their native languages, eat familiar foods, and surround themselves with kin and friends and people like them. It is no different for Americans when we live abroad. We congregate in enclaves, support shops that carry familiar foods like Skippy Peanut Butter, Rice Krispies, and Budweiser, build our own clubs, eat at American-style restaurants, and celebrate our holidays, like the Fourth of July and Thanksgiving, with other Americans, just as if we were at home. There are downsides to enclaves, however. Once established, enclaves can encourage additional immigration, reinforce the group's common identity, socialize the young into the subculture, and retard assimilation.[1]

When sociologists began studying ethnic neighborhoods and assimilation, they believed that ethnic segregation was an artifact of the low social status immigrants held in American society upon their arrival. Most sociologists thought that immigrant social status was temporary and that as an ethnic group's standing improved their enclaves would gradually disappear. Sociologists hypothesized the following four-stage process: (1) first-generation arrivals would seek cheap accommodations because of their poverty and desire to accumulate savings, and since the tenements adjacent to the city's center were cheap and close to jobs, they would become ethnic ghettoes; (2) children in the second generation would attend public schools, learn the language and the culture, and develop the skills needed for jobs of higher status, and over time incomes would rise, permitting these children of immigrants to pursue better housing and better neighborhoods, usually suburban; (3) the redistribution of the second generation into other areas of the city would lead to less ethnic segregation and a breakdown of the old cultural solidarity; the third generation would typically be English speakers and no longer know the mother tongue; and (4) subsequent movement would result in further dispersion of group members and their assimilation into the surrounding society. This is the pattern that social scientists have found. The descendants of third-wave immigrants live in more integrated neighborhoods than earlier generations, and this change in residential patters reflects how, in three generations, German, Irish, Italian, and Mexican immigrants have been transformed into Americans.[2]

The fourth wave is, however, more complicated and not yet fully understood. Remember that this current wave began in the 1970s, and a picture of their experiences is only now beginning to emerge. So far we know the following:

- The majority of current immigrants are settling in traditional gateway cities like New York, Chicago, San Francisco, Los Angeles, Dallas, and Houston, but millions more, mostly from Latin America, are moving to cities and small towns in nontraditional regions in the Midwest and South.[3]
- Asians recently passed Hispanics as the largest group of new immigrants to the United States. Foreign- and U.S.-born Asians now make up 5.8 percent of the U.S. population. Their education credentials are striking. More than 60 percent of Asian adults over the age of twenty-five have at least a bachelor's degree, and most are employed in highly skilled, high-paying professions. The trajectory of their assimilation will be much faster than other groups. Hispanics, in contrast, make up 16.6 percent of the population and have much lower levels of educational attainment, with the majority employed in low-skilled jobs.[4]
- The 2010 census reveals that Asian and Latino immigrants have moderate degrees of segregation, much lower than the segregation of blacks. Census data also show, however, that these patterns have been persistent and unchanged in the past three decades.[5]
- Hispanics are more highly segregated in the cities and small towns of the Midwest and South than they are in traditional gateway metros. Some researchers suggest that these residential patterns reflect hostility to the rapid economic and social changes associated with their influx into regions unaccustomed to large immigrant communities. Alabama's well-publicized anti-immigration climate is a good example.[6]
- The data gathered so far support the assimilation model. When the data are grouped by generation, second-generation Asians

and Hispanics are less segregated than the first generation, and subsequent generations have even lower levels of segregation.[7]

- Complicating the picture is the continuing migration of the fourth wave, which is replenishing ethnic enclaves with new immigrants. This ongoing movement masks assimilation that may have occurred. A recent announcement by Homeland Security suggests, however, that Hispanic migration may be ending, and this change may be reflected in the next census. The experiences of the fourth wave differ from the third wave's in that European immigration came to an abrupt end with the passage of the Immigration Act of 1924 and the advent of the Great Depression.

- Finally, fascinating new residential patterns are emerging in response to the fourth wave. About half of the population of multiethnic metros like Houston, Dallas, New York, Chicago, and Denver—home to 60 million Americans—live in neighborhoods with a complex array of whites, blacks, Hispanics, and Asians living together. Called *global neighborhoods,* these areas, first found in the 2000 census, represent a powerful new trend in America's racial and ethnic relations.[8]

Cities are where society meets the road. Changes taking place on the societal level are seen first and most clearly in the residential patterns in cities. The current wave of immigration is in its fourth decade, and most research supports the notion that immigrants are being successfully assimilated into American society. So, once again, the critics are wrong. Ethnic neighborhoods are playing their historical role of providing a haven for recently arrived immigrants. The integration of these groups into the urban fabric and their assimilation into our society are similar to the processes of earlier generations. Their residential patterns are different from those of the third wave because the automobile and a service economy shape today's cities. The process remains the same; the details of it are different.

Socioeconomic Integration

The United States has historically offered unparalleled economic opportunities to immigrants and their children, but the U.S. is unique in the world with the absence of federal programs aimed at integrating newcomers. This responsibility falls to families, schools, churches, and other local institutions, with the workplace being our most powerful integrating institution.

Immigrants make up a large and growing share of the U.S. labor force, and the numbers are now approaching rates last experienced during the peak of the third wave of immigration. Today, one in eight U.S. residents and one in six U.S. workers are foreign-born. Over the past two decades, immigrants have accounted for about half of the growth in the civilian labor force, and nearly one-fourth of U.S. youth projected to enter the labor force over the next decade have a foreign-born parent. Simply, immigrants and their children are the future of the American economy, and their integration into the workforce and society is vital to our future.[9]

Social scientists tend to gloss over the huge differences in class, race, ethnicity, and status among our immigrant population, but these factors shape its economic prospects and labor force integration. The degree of economic integration varies with immigrant workers' education, skill levels, language abilities, lengths of residence, and immigration statuses. Some immigrant groups fare better than the U.S.-born, and others fare worse. The experiences of Asian and Hispanic immigrants are instructive.

In 1965 the Asian American share of the U.S. population stood at less than 1 percent. The Immigration Act of 1924 prescribed quotas that effectively kept Asian immigrants out. Today, Asians make up nearly 6 percent of the U.S. population, and this growth is recent—74 percent of Asian American adults are foreign born. In addition, in a knowledge- and information-based economy, Asian Americans have excelled because they have the education and skills tailor-made for the global economy. Nearly half of Asian American adults have a college degree (compared with 28 percent of the overall U.S. population); over half report that they speak English very well; and the vast majority (93 percent) believe hard work pays off. Asian Americans place a strong emphasis on education, careers, and family, and they have been remarkably successful in their adopted society. Many work in management, technology, and professional jobs, an employment pattern reflected in their median household income of $66,000, far larger than the $49,800 for all U.S. households.[10]

In contrast, the Hispanic American's share of the U.S. population is 16 percent, making it the nation's largest ethnic or racial minority. Nearly two-thirds of Hispanics in the United States self-identify as being of Mexican origin. Their most recent immigration is in its fourth decade, and the children and grandchildren of the immigrant generation now define their group: 74 percent of Hispanics are citizens, and only 26 percent are foreign-born. In sharp contrast with Asians, only 13 percent of Hispanics have a college degree, and only 63 percent report that they speak English very well. Although Hispanics, like Asians, have a strong work ethic, their lower overall levels of education mean most jobs are in the low-paying sector of the labor market, and they have a median family income of $40,200.[11]

So does socioeconomic integration follow the assimilation model? Most research shows that the socioeconomic status of second- and third-generation immigrants, regardless of their race and ethnicity, is higher than that of the first generation. Looking at only education, the experiences of the second generation are striking. For example, researchers found that only 40 percent of first-generation Hispanic immigrants arriving in the 1980s had high school degrees, but twenty years later, the percentage for their children had jumped to 85 percent. Among Asians the data are even more striking. The second generation of Asians are far outpacing the societal average in nearly all measures of socioeconomic attainment.[12]

As with the other measures of assimilation, research shows that our most recent immigrants are being integrated into the economic and social fabric of this society. The recent recession and the weak recovery could change the economic and social forces that have historically propelled the intergenerational mobility of immigrants and native-born Americans alike. As the U.S. economy completes its shift from a manufacturing to an information-based economy, the labor market will place a premium on those who are highly skilled and educated, leading to an increased inequality and declining wages among the unskilled in our society. This is another compelling reason for the passage of the DREAM Act. Our society can ill afford to squander the skills and talents of a generation of children and young adults.

Language

More than thirty years ago the Supreme Court in *Plyler v. Doe* recognized our national interest in providing undocumented children a public education. The court viewed K–12 education for all children, regardless of immigration status, as vital to our democracy because it prevented the emergence of a permanent underclass, and it gave all children the promise of full participation in our society. The role of education is as important now as it was then. It is the way the children of immigrants learn English. It is essential in the assimilation process because Americans believe that speaking the English language is a key component of national identity—it is the social glue that holds our 315 million people together. A recent national poll showed that 94 percent of Americans believe that being able to speak English should be important or very important in determining if someone is a true American.

It should come as no surprise that English usage is a hot-button issue in the immigration debate. In 1981 Virginia declared English the official state language, and twenty-seven states passed similar measures in subsequent decades. In the run-up to the passage of anti-immigration laws in Arizona and Alabama, English usage was a key issue. Despite the sometimes shrill nature of public debates on English-only and bilingual education, multiculturalism, and language competency, the evidence of language assimilation of the current wave is quite good.

In fact, immigrants are learning English faster than the large waves of immigrants who came to the United States at the turn of the twentieth century. Fewer than half of all immigrants who arrived in the United States between 1900 and 1920 spoke English within their first five years after immigrating, whereas more than three-quarters who arrived between 1980 and 2000 spoke English within the first five years.[13]

The shift from a mother tongue to English is particularly striking when looking at language shifts across generations. The proportion who speak only English or who speak English very well jumps to more than 80 percent by the second generation for Hispanic, Asian, and other groups. By the third and subsequent generations, close to everyone, regardless of ethnic heritage, reports speaking only English or speaking it well.[14] Thus, the three-generation model of language assimilation appears to hold for immigrants who entered at the turn of the twentieth century and those who arrived at its end. The immigrant generation makes some progress but remains dominant in their native tongue; the second generation is bilingual; and the third generation usually speaks only English. Once again, the evidence shows that the critics are wrong—our newest immigrants are rapidly assimilating into the social fabric of American society.[15]

Intermarriage

Intermarriage is a hot-button issue among many anti-immigrant organizations, like the American Immigration Control Foundation and NumbersUSA, which link race with intelligence and blame immigrants for many American social problems. To them intermarriage means the end of American society, but to social scientists intermarriage is the ultimate proof of assimilation. When individuals marry outside their racial or ethnic groups, there is strong evidence that the social barriers to these marriages were thin. For the marriage market to work, couples need opportunities to meet and fall in love, and these opportunities are tied to where people live, work, shop, attend school, and spend their leisure time. The modest levels of segregation among Hispanic and Asian immigrants, along with the emergence of global neighborhoods in our most ethnically diverse metros, mean lots of chance and informal meetings among Asians, Hispanics, whites, and blacks, creating conditions ripe for romantic love and intermarriage.

The Pew Research Center published "The Rise of Intermarriage" in 2012, which finds the following:

- Almost 15 percent of all new marriages in the United States in 2010 were between spouses of different races or ethnicities, more than doubling the rate in the 1980s. Approximately 26 percent of Hispanics and 28 percent of Asians married outside their ethnic group between 2008 and 2010.
- Western states top the intermarriage rate in the United States, with more than 20 percent of all newlyweds having married someone of a different race or ethnicity between 2008 and 2010. Other regions had lower rates: the South was at 14 percent; the Northeast, 13 percent; and the Midwest, 11 percent. The findings are not surprising given the large concentration

of Asians and Hispanics in the West—there simply was more opportunity.

- Intermarriage rates between whites and Asians and Latinos are much higher than among whites and blacks.
- One-third of Americans say that a member of their immediate family or a close relative is married to someone of a different race. Nearly two-thirds of Americans say it would be "fine with them" if a family member married someone outside the family's racial or ethnic group.
- On the topic of intermarriage, 43 percent of Americans believe it is a change for the better in our society; 44 percent say that it makes no difference; and only 11 percent say it makes our society worse. Americans' favorable attitudes about intermarriage have grown significantly in the past twenty-five years.[16]

The press has pounced on the anti-immigration fervor in Arizona, Alabama, and other states and suggested that impermeable barriers exist between whites and the current wave of immigrants. The reality is the opposite. Intermarriage rates between these groups suggest that social barriers between ethnic groups are, as mentioned, quite thin. And once again, our immigrant history seems to be repeating itself. Italians in the first half of the twentieth century out-married at about the same rate that Mexicans of the same generation did at the end of the twentieth century.[17] And there are other similarities, as well. Now, as in our past, there is significant intermarriage within our broad ethnic groups—Asian, European, and Hispanic—yielding panethnic unions, as in a Chinese person marrying a Korean or a Cuban marrying a Guatemalan or, fifty years ago, an Italian marrying a Greek. The higher rates of intermarriage within these broad categories suggest these categories are meaningful in how individuals select their mates.[18]

Marriage is the most intimate relationship that we can enter into during our lives, and intermarriage is the bellwether of assimilation. As with their other criticisms, opponents of immigration have gotten it wrong again. Whether it be where current immigrants live; their education levels, jobs, and incomes; or their mastery of English, the current wave of immigrants is assimilating at a rate as fast as that of the earlier European wave.

Final Thoughts

In the past five years of conducting research on my region's Hispanic community, I have observed the assimilation process firsthand. Sixty-six thousand Hispanics, along with a growing number of Asians and Marshall Islanders, call northwest Arkansas home. Most of our *new* residents live in enclaves, and grocery stores, churches, restaurants, clinics, and an array of professionals have sprung up to serve the needs of their communities. As a sociologist I find these neighborhoods fascinating, and as a resident I feel they add to the tang, thrill, and enjoyment of our community's life. In addition, these enclaves play their historical function in the integration of our newest residents into our communities and their assimilation into our society. I have been lucky to watch this process.

Critics of immigration and the DREAM Act fear what they do not know. As I researched this chapter, I wondered how they could have gotten things so wrong. Regardless of the measure of assimilation, whether residential and socioeconomic integration or language acquisition and intermarriage, all show rapid assimilation across all groups. The three-generation assimilation model well described the groups that arrived at the turn of the twentieth century, as well as the groups that arrived at the end of that century. Earlier waves have expanded our economy, built a great nation, and enriched the American culture. Why would we think it would be otherwise with our newest arrivals?

There is a certain irony that the newest wave of immigration is assimilating far faster than the groups that arrived earlier—the ancestors of the critics. But the critics need not fear our newest groups, because, as I have shown, they are fitting into our existing social structure and culture. They are learning English; they are embracing our values; they are upwardly mobile; and they are coming to this country for the same reasons as past generations: for the freedom, liberty, and economic opportunities found here.

In 2012 Gallup reported that 66 percent of Americans thought immigration was a good thing for the country, up from 59 percent in the previous year, and this change in immigration views was across political parties. Perhaps it is time for our politicians to stop listening to a vocal minority, begin to address immigration reform in ways that the majority of Americans support, and, like our president, have the courage to do what is right: allowing undocumented children and young adults to stay in this country, permitting them to go to school and work, providing them with a path to citizenship, and giving them the opportunity to contribute to our society.

PART 2

The DREAM Act, DREAMers, and America's Future

SIX

The DREAM Act
Nuts and Bolts

President Obama's June 15, 2012 bombshell announcement that deportation rules will be eased to allow some young undocumented immigrants to remain in the United States was received by DREAMers with a mixture of joy, relief, hope, incredulity, caution, and distrust. Minutes after hearing the announcement, I e-mailed the young people I had been working with and asked, "What was your reaction to president's announcement?" Jazmin wrote the following:

> I was shocked, my heart was pounding, I wondered if I had wandered off into an alternate universe where it was possible to dare think that I might have a real shot at getting papers.
>
> A friend called me when I got to my office and congratulated me, and I had no idea why. When I found out, I just went crazy and started pulling up every online article I could and posting them on Facebook, calling up my brother, my sister, my undergrad adviser . . . it was a very happy morning. I watched the official announcement from the White House later that day and shared my story with some of the other students in my office for the first time. I was very relieved to hear that they supported a policy like this.
>
> It changes my outlook and plans. I have some real hope of being able to get my PhD in this country now . . . I had really dreaded the prospect of leaving. I'm looking forward to getting my driver's license and being able to be a teaching assistant.

Looking over the dozens of e-mails that I received, however, their overall tone can best be described as cautiously celebratory. My phone conversation with Rafael, a DREAMer activist, a few hours after the president's press conference captures this mood:

> Of course, we are all thrilled. But we have heard promises before. I've talked and messaged dozens of DREAMers and most are celebrating, but I think it's premature because this policy is very similar to what we've seen in the past. . . . It's not a law. There're no details on how it's going to be enforced. . . . We've seen how prosecutorial discretion has worked in the past, and lots of undocumented have been screwed. We're not going to stop fighting until it is implemented.

Why the concern? Why the trepidation? What exactly did Secretary of Homeland Security Janet Napolitano announce? Her press release is as follows:

> Effective immediately, certain young people who were brought to the United States as young children, do not present a risk to national security or public safety, and meet several key criteria will be considered for relief from removal from the country or from entering into removal proceedings. Those who demonstrate that they meet the criteria will be eligible to receive deferred action for a period of two years, subject to renewal, and will be eligible to apply for work authorization.

Under this directive, individuals must meet the following criteria.

1. Came to the United States under the age of sixteen;

2. Have continuously resided in the United States for at least five years preceding the date of this memorandum and are present in the United States on the date of this memorandum;

3. Are currently in school, have graduated from high school, have obtained a general education development certificate, or are honorably discharged veterans of the Coast Guard or Armed Forces of the United States;

4. Have not been convicted of a felony offense, a significant misdemeanor offense, multiple misdemeanor offenses, or otherwise pose a threat to national security or public safety;

5. Are not above the age of thirty.[1]

THE DREAM ACT

This is not amnesty. It does not require congressional approval. Deferred action will be administratively implemented on a case-by-case basis. Although, under this new policy, as many as 1.4 million unauthorized youth could gain relief from deportation, the real number will probably be lower.[2]

On the positive side, the new policy allows the undocumented to act proactively. They can apply before they are arrested and caught up in the deportation process. A two-year period of deferred action will be granted to successful applicants, and if it is granted, many will be eligible for work permits. It also appears that there will be greater fairness, since the department's U.S. Citizenship and Immigration Services (USCIS), which is tasked with reviewing benefits and not enforcement, will review the applications.

But immigration reform advocates have serious concerns. First, this is not an executive order; rather, it is a policy directive granting only deferred action.[3] The Department of Homeland Security (DHS) can deny an application even if the applicant meets the eligibility criteria, and there is no right to appeal. Even if granted, a person's deferred action can be terminated at any time without review.[4]

Second, many people may be deported simply for applying. If an undocumented youth's application is denied, his or her case may be referred to Immigration and Custom's Enforcement (ICE) for deportation. Since there is no due process, administrative mistakes can go uncorrected.

Third, the clause "significant misdemeanor offense and multiple misdemeanor offenses" is troubling. A local immigration lawyer tells me that she worries many young people could be denied deferred action for offenses like driving without a license, truancy, or other minor offenses. She says, "If you are undocumented and live in Springdale with its frequent ICE sweeps and police traffic stops, you're bound to have several misdemeanors on your record."[5]

Fourth and more troubling, ICE has a history of ignoring directives. In June 2011, John Morton, the director of ICE, ordered his deportation officers to prioritize enforcement "on the exercise of prosecutorial discretion to ensure that the agency's immigration enforcement resources were focused on 19 priorities."[6] Many agency personnel ignored his directive. Since the Obama administration has insulated

DHS's new policy from judicial review, there is no mechanism for holding DHS or its agencies accountable.[7]

I have my own additional concerns. First, undocumented children and youth will continue to live a life of uncertainty with reprieves coming in two-year installments. Second, there is no path to citizenship; undocumented youth remain in limbo. Although President Obama's order is an important first step, the nation still needs the Congress to pass the DREAM Act, and comprehensive immigration reform remains vital to the nation and its economy.

Although Secretary Napolitano's policy directive of deferred action shares many similarities with the DREAM Act, there are important differences. The DREAM Act is designed to allow undocumented immigrant youth who were brought to the United States as children to obtain conditional lawful permanent resident (LPR) status if they remain in high school, receive a degree (or GED), and go on to college or join the military. The current version of the DREAM Act would permit students to obtain conditional LPR status if they satisfied the following conditions:

- They entered the United States before the age of sixteen and are under thirty-five on the date of the bill's enactment.
- They have been continuously present in the country for at least five years prior to the bill's enactment.
- They have obtained a high school degree or a GED.
- They can demonstrate good moral character.

Undocumented students who satisfied these conditions would be able to apply for six-year conditional legal permanent status, which would allow them to work, travel, attend college, or join the military. If, within this six-year period, an undocumented youth completed at least two years toward a four-your degree, graduated from a two-year college, or served at least two years in the military and maintained good moral character, the conditional status would be removed and the person would be granted permanent resident status and eligible for U.S. citizenship. In the bill's latest version, DREAM Act students would not be eligible for federal grants but could participate in federal work study and student loan programs and qualify for in-state tuition and state-funded financial aid.[8]

The Department of Homeland Security's new policy, in contrast, does not provide conditional LPR. It instead puts undocumented youth on a two-year review cycle. Although it removes the immediate threat of deportation for thousands of young people, their futures remain uncertain. Questions remain. How will DHS implement President Obama and Secretary Napolitano's policy? Will eligible students time out now that the maximum age has been reduced from thirty-five to thirty? More important, the thrust of the DREAM Act is on education and human-capital development. Supporters of the legislation recognize our society's investment in the K–12 and college education of undocumented youth. The DREAM Act is not an order to cease or to defer action—it provides a way to tap talents and skills through a path to citizenship.[9]

Plyler v. Doe Revisited

Behind the political posturing of Congress over the access of the undocumented to higher education looms *Plyler v. Doe,* the landmark Supreme Court case that has framed this education debate.[10] Justice Brennan's words ring as true today as when they were written:

> Education provides the basic tools by which individuals might lead economically productive lives to the benefit of us all. In sum, education has a fundamental role in maintaining the fabric of our society. We cannot ignore the significant social costs borne by our Nation when select groups are denied the means to absorb the values and skills upon which our societal order rests.

Nearly two generations of undocumented children have benefited from the *Plyler* ruling. These children have been educated in American schools, raised in our communities, and socialized into our society. As I show in Chapter 4, they embrace our values and our aspirations. They are American in every way except immigration status. Generation 1.5 is caught in the middle, and our treatment of these young people defies logic. Although the Obama administration has aggressively enforced immigration statutes and has deported a record number of unauthorized immigrants, the reality is that his and past administrations have deported few of our 2.1 million undocumented youth. Given the shift in DHS policy, even fewer undocumented youth will be deported. The reality is that most will live their lives in our society. Doesn't it make sense to invest in and use their talents and skills?[11]

Because of *Plyler*, undocumented youth are able to receive free public education through high school in the United States. The ruling, however, left open the question as to what should happen when undocumented students apply to state-supported colleges and universities. In 1996, in response to a growing number of unauthorized immigrants, Congress passed and President Clinton signed two laws, the Illegal Immigration Reform and Immigrant Responsibility Act (IIRIRA) and the Personal Responsibility and Work Opportunity Act (PRWORA). Together, they severely limit the ability of undocumented immigrants to receive government services. The laws prohibit states from granting unauthorized youth postsecondary educational benefits on the basis of state residence unless equal benefits are made available to all U.S. citizens. This prohibition is commonly understood to apply to the granting of in-state tuition. In addition, the laws make undocumented youth ineligible for federal financial aid, prohibit them from working legally, and make them subject to deportation.

The DREAM Act repeals Section 505 of IIRIRA, allowing states to grant higher education benefits, including in-state tuition, to undocumented students. The DREAM Act extends the educational benefits of *Plyler v. Doe* to postsecondary education, restores a state's right to establish its own criteria in determining who qualifies for in-state tuition and other state educational benefits, and protects our society's investment in the education of undocumented youth by providing a path to citizenship.

Senators Orrin Hatch (R-UT) and Richard Durbin (D-IL) introduced the DREAM Act in 2001. Since then, multiple DREAM Act bills have been introduced to address the plight of undocumented students, and most have proposed the two-pronged approach I describe. In July 2003 Senators Hatch and Durbin reintroduced the legislation with strong bipartisan support (there were forty-eight cosponsors from both parties), but the bill never made it to the Senate floor for a vote. In the House, 152 members on both sides of the aisle sponsored a similar bill. In the 111th Congress, the House approved DREAM Act language in an unrelated bill, but that bill failed in the Senate on a 55–41 vote, five votes short of invoking cloture. The bill died at the end of the Congress. The 112th Congress ended on January 3, 2013. During the session, legislation in both the House and the Senate was introduced with bipartisan cosponsorship (H 1842 and S 952), but the DREAM Act failed to pass.[12]

Support for the DREAM Act remains high among the general electorate. Even in Arizona, polling released in April 2012 shows that nearly three-quarters of Arizona's registered voters support the DREAM Act. In addition, an NBC News/*Wall Street Journal* poll released a month later shows almost 70 percent of Americans favoring the Obama administration's new immigration policy toward DREAM-eligible youth. Support in the Hispanic and Asian communities is overwhelming. A December 2011 poll by the Pew Hispanic Center shows 91 percent of Hispanics supporting the DREAM Act.[13] Many of the nation's labor, political, and business organizations have also rallied support for the legislation. Congress simply is out of touch with the American people. With Congress in gridlock and with historically low approval ratings, it is not surprising that the states have taken up the cause of undocumented youth.

States Take Up the DREAM Act

Most of the supporting arguments for in-state tuition for the undocumented reflect points raised in Justice Brennan's *Plyler* opinion. First, undocumented students who arrived as minors should not be punished for the unlawful behavior of their parents. Second, many undocumented youth drop out of school because they know they cannot afford out-of-state tuition. This financial reality is psychologically damaging to students, and the result is a waste of their skills and talents. Third, the students want to live in the United States and have no intention of leaving. They've been taught in school, just like their American classmates, that a college education is a prerequisite for high-paying jobs. College graduates make more money, contribute more to the economy, and pay more taxes. Finally, with hope for a future, more undocumented youth will graduate from high school, more will pursue a college degree or enter the military, and more will become self-sufficient adults—all outcomes that will lower social service costs.[14]

To date, the legislators of one-third of the states have found these arguments compelling, and have used Section 505 of IIRIRA to justify their legislation:

> An alien who is not lawfully present in the United States shall not be eligible on the basis of residence within a State (or a political subdivision) for any postsecondary education benefit *unless* a citizen or national of the United States is eligible for such benefit. (italics added)[15]

Contrary to the claims of the critics, states are not using a loophole in federal law to give in-state benefits. The law is very specific. Section 505 of IIRIRA prohibits states from providing any higher education benefit based on residence to undocumented immigrants unless they provide the same benefit to U.S. citizens in the same circumstances, regardless of their residence. Congress could have prohibited these benefits, but they chose not to.

The states that provide in-state tuition benefits generally require the students to have (1) attended a school in the state for a certain number of years; (2) graduated from high school in the state; and (3) signed an affidavit stating that they either have applied to legalize their status or will do so as soon as eligible. Note that there is no mention of residency. U.S. citizens and the undocumented are eligible for the benefit. For example, in Texas nonresidents would be eligible for in-state tuition if they attended a private boarding school in Texas that enrolled out-of-state students. If the school provided grades 9–12 education and the students spent their high school career in the state and graduated, they would be eligible for in-state tuition even though their families have residency elsewhere. Alternatively, if students in another DREAM Act state, say Missouri, graduated from a state high school but their families moved out of state, assuming they met the state's other criteria, they would be eligible for in-state tuition. Again, the benefit would not be based on residency.[16]

Fourteen states currently have laws or policies permitting certain undocumented students who have graduated from their high schools to pay in-state tuition. These states are California, Connecticut, Illinois, Kansas, Maryland, Nebraska, New Mexico, New York, Oklahoma, Texas, Utah, and Washington. In addition, Rhode Island's Board of Governors for Higher Education unanimously voted to provide access to in-state tuition, regardless of immigration status, beginning in 2012. In November 2012, Massachusetts's governor issued an executive order granting undocumented youth in-state tuition as soon as they received worker permits through deferred action. California has by far the largest number (28.7 percent) of potential beneficiaries, followed by Texas (13.7 percent), Florida (8.7 percent), Arizona (6.3 percent), and New York (4.1 percent). Together, they account for 62 percent of those eligible for relief under the DREAM Act.[17]

How Many Undocumented Would Be Eligible?

The Migration Policy Institute (MPI) is a nonpartisan organization that analyzes international migration policies. In 2010 MPI published *DREAM vs. Reality: An Analysis of Potential DREAM Act Beneficiaries*.[18] Using public government data, they estimated that approximately 2.1 million undocumented children and young people could qualify for legalization through the DREAM Act (see Table 1). They concluded, however, that only 825,000 (38 percent) would have a reasonable chance of obtaining permanent residency under the law. Factors like English-language ability, income/poverty status, presence of dependent children, and employment status would be potent barriers to achieving the requirements of the law. The researchers combined potential beneficiaries into four groups and applied historic education, labor force, income, and demographic data to come up with their estimates.

Group 1 comprises the undocumented ages eighteen to thirty-four who have at least an associate's degree (plus retroactively eligible adults over age thirty-five). MPI reasoned that this group would be the least likely to encounter barriers, because they had met all requirements. They estimated that 114,000 (100 percent) would qualify for permanent residency.

Group 2 is made up of the undocumented youth ages eighteen to thirty-four who have only a high school degree or a GED. In order to qualify for the benefits of the DREAM Act, they must meet the minimum two-year higher educational or military requirement while exhibiting good moral character. The researchers reasoned that this group would experience significant barriers in meeting the educational requirement

Table 1: Potential and Estimated Dream Act Beneficiaries by Group According to MPI

	Number of Potential Beneficiaries	Number Estimated to Gain Residency (percent)
Group 1: Eligible for permanent status • 18–34 with at least an associate's degree • 35 or older with at least an associate's degree (under retroactive benefits)	114,000	114,000 (100)
Group 2: Eligible for conditional status • 18–34 with high school diploma or GED	612,000	290,000 (47)
Group 3: Eligible in the future if they obtain a high school degree • Children under 18	934,000	400,000 (43)
Group 4: Not eligible for conditional status unless they obtain a GED • 18–34 with no high school degree	489,000	22,000 (4)
	2,150,000	825,000

Source: Jeanne Batalova and Margie McHugh, "Dream vs. Reality: An Analysis of Potential DREAM Act Beneficiaries," *Insight*, Migration Policy Institute website, July 2010, http://www.migrationpolicy.org/pubs/DREAM-Insight-July2010.pdf.

and that only 260,000 undocumented would qualify (the number grows to 290,000 with the 30,000 who would qualify through military service). Therefore, only 47 percent (290,000) of the 612,000 potential beneficiaries would be expected to qualify for permanent residency.

Group 3, children under age eighteen, would confront even greater challenges because its undocumented youth lack the conditional status requirement of a high school degree or a GED. These children would have to complete at least two years of college or two years of military duty while facing English-language, poverty, and educational-cost barriers. Considering all of these obstacles, MPI estimated that only 400,000 (43 percent) of the 934,000 potential beneficiaries would qualify.

Group 4, undocumented youth ages eighteen to thirty-four without a high school diploma, would be expected to have the lowest permanent residency attainment rates. MPI believes their barriers would be overwhelming, and only 22,000 (4 percent) of 489,000 potential beneficiaries would be able to change their immigration status under this legislation.

Implementation of the DREAM Act at the federal level would have state-level consequences. College enrollment and tuition policies vary by state and campus, so access to education would significantly vary from state to state. The act would have the greatest impact on states with large undocumented populations, so a student living in California or Texas would have a far better chance for higher education than a student in, for instance, Alabama.

How Much Would It Cost?

Critics of in-state tuition policies, like FAIR and the Center for Immigration Studies (CIS), claim that the DREAM Act would be a financial burden. The reports issued by these organizations frequently suffer, however, from the severe methodological shortcomings I have discussed. A more sound way to measure the financial impact of the DREAM Act on state budgets would be (1) analyzing the true costs of providing instruction; (2) calculating the revenue generated by in-state tuition paid by undocumented students, minus the revenue lost if they were paying nonresident tuition; (3) calculating the net cost of education by subtracting costs minus revenues; and (4) comparing the net costs with long-term benefits (e.g., students' future financial contributions to states' economies and the increased tax base provided if these youth were college graduates rather than high school graduates or dropouts). This scheme looks at the DREAM Act as an investment in the future.

Studies at the federal and the state levels show that the DREAM Act is good public policy. The benefits would far exceed the costs of its programs, and the contributions of college-educated people to the economy and tax base would be in the trillions of dollars. For example, a 2010 study by the nonpartisan Congressional Budget Office estimates that if Congress approved the DREAM Act, 2.6 million jobs would be created and the federal budget would see a net increase of $1.4 billion over the first ten years of the program.[19] A study using the aforementioned MPI data found that if the 825,000 individuals likely to apply for and obtain benefits under the DREAM Act graduated, they would generate an additional $1.4 trillion in both economic activity and taxes over a forty-year career.[20]

These are national data, however. How would the measure affect states? It is estimated that only 65,000 undocumented students graduate from our nation's high schools each year. The experiences of Texas, California, Massachusetts, New York, and other states show that only a small number of undocumented high school graduates take advantage of in-state tuition benefits when offered. Although California has the nation's largest number of undocumented students, the state estimates that only 1,620 undocumented students took advantage of the state's DREAM Act in 2007.[21] Most states would be providing in-state tuition to only a few thousand undocumented youth, and in Arkansas it would be a few hundred. A North Carolina study reports that if the state allowed undocumented immigrants to attend college at in-state tuition rates, then "North Carolina stands to gain $28 million in additional tax revenue as a result of just one year of the program implementation. . . . Total lifetime benefits to program participants would be more than $406 million."[22]

Critics of the DREAM Act argue that these students should pay out-of-state tuition because far more revenue would be generated. Their argument is based on the faulty assumption that these students can afford to pay out-of-state tuition. In Arkansas the difference between in-state and out-of-state tuition is over $9,000 annually, and in my interviews with the undocumented, I found that most had been priced out of college on our campus. In truth, in-state tuition more than covers the marginal cost of enrolling a small number of undocumented students. Since the first twenty students who enroll in a class usually cover its costs, additional enrollment would mean more money for the general fund.

For example, the University of Arkansas offers the New Arkansan Scholarship Award, which provides in-state tuition to out-of-state students who demonstrate high academic achievement. The university closely analyzed the financial impact of the program "to make certain that non-resident students would bring income to the university and the state—not drain resources." The program has not drained resources. Since the program's inception, "the university has realized net revenue from the program that is one-and-a-half times greater than [it] realized before the policy was put into effect." If the state passed the DREAM Act, the additional students would "add marginally to [the university's] fixed costs . . . but . . . contribute substantially to [its] savings."[23] Income from the scholarship program has been a new revenue stream for the university and has provided money for raises, student programs, and campus improvements. If this experience were to hold true in other states, then state-supported universities would have a lot to lose by denying in-state tuition to undocumented students.

Would the DREAM Act Work?

In an effort to assess the impact of DREAM Act passage at the state level, the nonpartisan Latino Policy Institute at Roger Williams University in Rhode Island conducted a systematic review of available research and found the following: (1) the passage of a state DREAM Act resulted in an average 31 percent increase in noncitizen enrollment in college; (2) some schools experienced growth as high as 54 percent in noncitizen enrollment after passage; (3) providing in-state tuition resulted in an average 14 percent decrease in noncitizen high school dropout rates; and (4) in-state tuition legislation did not appear to have a financial cost to the implementing states. Therefore, available research suggests that in-state tuition legislation improves educational outcomes by reducing high school dropout rates and increasing enrollment in institutes of higher education. Their report concludes, "This systematic review of available literature gives reason to believe that the passage of in-state tuition legislation would be a benefit to Rhode Island—economically, socially, and educationally."[24]

Yes, the DREAM Act has the desired policy outcome: these laws significantly affect the decisions of undocumented students to go to college by lowering the financial barriers to higher education. If the DREAM Act were to become federal law, then a significant number of our nation's undocumented youth would have a meaningful chance to receive a college degree and permanent residential status. In particular, it would give hope for a future in this society to nearly one million K–12 students. Rhode Island's DREAM Act has benefitted the state economically, socially, and educationally. Imagine the positive impact on all undocumented youth if the DREAM Act were passed at the federal level.

What Would Be the DREAM Act's Benefits?

The DREAM act would give beneficiaries access to greater educational opportunities and better jobs, which, in turn, would mean more taxable income. Studies on the undocumented immigrants who received legal status under the 1986 Immigration Reform and Control Act found that these legalized immigrants experienced significant upward mobility, increasing their income by 15 percent in the first five years. Simply, given the opportunity immigrants, now and throughout our history, have improved their education and skills, gotten better jobs, spent more, invested more, and paid more taxes. This is the American Dream, one shared by the DREAMers.

Researchers have shown in hundreds of studies the strong link between education and income. The average college graduate earns 60 percent more than a high school graduate, and advanced degrees have an even higher payoff.[25] Income isn't the only benefit. These jobs typically come with health and life insurance, retirement plans, and other benefits. A 2010 study by the North American Integration and Development Center found that if the DREAM Act became law, the participants would increase their incomes from between $1.4 to $3.6 trillion over a forty-year career. These staggering sums would contribute to our economy and benefit us all.

The DREAM Act would allow legalized immigrants to invest in the U.S. economy. Uncertainty and investments are a bad mix. I discovered this in my interview with Juan, an Arkansas DREAMer activist. Undocumented and cut off from the labor market, Juan opened his first business at fifteen. Today, at twenty-four, he owns a thriving company that has a growing number of employees, and the irony is that he's the only undocumented person in the company. He maintains a payroll; remains current with local, state, and federal taxes; and pays good wages. He continues to add workers and is helping to grow our region's economy. What I did not know until our interview was that if he were arrested, he would lose everything through the deportation process—his business and assets would be confiscated by ICE.

A Center for American Progress and Immigration Policy Center study shows that legalizing the roughly 11 million undocumented immigrants through comprehensive immigration reform would grow the economy by $1.5 trillion over ten years, boost wages for native-born and newly legalized immigrants, and lay the foundation for robust, just, and widespread economic growth. Removing uncertainty and the threat of deportation and stopping the confiscation of homes, automobiles, and companies mean that the undocumented would invest more in our neighborhoods, communities, and nation. We all would benefit.[26]

The DREAM Act would contribute to our knowledge- and information-based economy and keep talented students in the United States. The skills, talents, educations, and entrepreneurial spirits of our people will determine the nation's share of the global economy. In a knowledge- and information-based global economy, our nation's most important investment is in our human capital. A lack of hope and an uncertain future mean that only 5 to 10 percent of undocumented youth go to college. The promise of potential doctors, lawyers, scientists, teachers, and other professionals is not being realized. We are squandering important assets.

At a more basic level, immigrants make up a large and growing share of the U.S. labor force. The number of immigrants in the labor force is now approaching levels last seen at the turn of the twentieth century. As the baby boom generation retires, immigrants and their children will assume a critical role in sustaining the U.S. economy in an ever-competitive global market. The demographic reality is that we need their labor.[27]

The DREAM Act would save taxpayers money by reducing the high school dropout rate and lowering social service costs. A RAND study shows that raising Hispanics' college graduation rate would increase education spending by 10 percent but that the cost would be more than offset by savings in public services. States with DREAM Acts have experienced significant reductions in high school dropout rates, and, therefore, lower social service costs.[28]

The DREAM Act would help universities. Universities are seeing the end of the millennial generation, and the number of youth graduating from our nation's high schools is on the decline. By granting academically gifted undocumented youth access to college, university administrators would be tapping underused capacity, and these youth could provide an important new revenue source. With its in-state tuition scholarship for high-ability nonresident students, the University of Arkansas has the data to support this idea.

The DREAM Act would help revitalize our cities. Baltimore, Chicago, Dayton, Detroit, New York, St. Louis, and a growing number of U.S. cities are courting immigrants to reverse a half-century of population decline. Often older metropolitan areas with Rust Belt manufacturing economies, these cities' newest residents have helped revitalize inner-city neighborhoods and expand local economies. For example, Detroit helps immigrants start small businesses, get driver's licenses, and learn English. Other cities sponsor soccer programs, library programs for immigrant children, and health and dental care. Baltimore's mayor, Stephanie Rawlings-Blake, has told immigrant groups that she is "counting on them to help Baltimore gain 10,000 families in the next decade."[29] Immigration reform means that the historic role of immigrants building, growing, and revitalizing our cities will continue with the fourth wave.

The DREAM Act would give us a competitive edge in a global economy. DREAMers are from not only Central and South America but also dozens of countries outside those regions. DREAMers usually know their native languages and cultures and, equally important, have social networks here and abroad. Employing people who can navigate another society and use their connections to introduce companies into new markets are important competitive advantages in a global economy.

The DREAM Act would aid military recruiting. The twin pillars of America's national security are a strong economy and a strong military. I have shown the DREAM Act's potential for strengthening our economy. The average age of a white American is forty-seven, and the average age of an immigrant is twenty-seven. The stark demographic reality is that our military must tap this manpower in order to maintain our national defense.[30]

The DREAM Act would contribute to the solvency of Social Security and Medicare. A June 8, 2012, opinion piece in the *Washington Post,* "Baby Boomers Had Better Embrace Change," explores the relationship between the 78 million baby boomers and the growing importance of first- and second-generation immigration to our society, labor force, and economy.[31] The message to my generation was stark: "It is this diverse youth population [of immigrants] that the largely white baby boomers will rely upon in their retirement years to keep paying into Social Security and Medicare." Demographic patterns are the foundation of any society, determining its future and potential. The bottom line is that our society depends on the fortune of our growing immigrant population. We had better embrace it.

Final Thoughts

Studies show time and time again that legal status brings fiscal, economic, and labor market benefits to individual immigrants, to their families, and to our society. Over time, given the opportunity our undocumented youth will improve their educations, find better jobs, earn more, spend more, and contribute to a growing economy and a larger tax base. As I have shown, the number of undocumented youth is small, around 65,000 high school graduates per year, and when we compare this number with the millions who yearly attend two- and four-year colleges and universities, the cost of passing the DREAM Act would be insignificant. Although the DREAMers' numbers are small, they can make a positive long-term impact on our workforce, our military, our safety net programs, and our economic growth.

SEVEN

Meet Two DREAMers

U nlike the governments in other developed nations, the U.S. federal government plays a minor role in the assimilation of immigrants into our society. This responsibility falls to local communities and their neighborhoods, churches, schools, and workplaces. Perhaps surprisingly, this arrangement works well. Last year, the nation's Hispanic college student population reached a record high, exceeding 2 million—a record 16.5 percent of all college enrollments—and the data for Asian college students were even better.[1] As a result, the nation's colleges and universities are playing an increasingly important role in preparing the next generation of professionals and leaders among our fourth wave of immigrants.

The Pew Hispanic Center estimates that 2.1 million undocumented youth from around the world live in the United States, and an increasing number of them attend U.S. colleges and universities. The undocumented are indistinguishable from other students on campus, but they find themselves in a double bind. Until the Department of Homeland Security (DHS) announced their deferred action policy, most lived in the shadows. Nonresident tuition meant they could afford only one or two classes a semester, and they balanced school with family and jobs in the informal economy.

My research for this book began in August 2011, when I attended a workshop sponsored by the University of Arkansas's United We Dream affiliate. DREAMers from Texas, Oklahoma, Kansas, Missouri, and Arkansas attended the two-day conference. On the first day, each state's delegates reported their legislative challenges and the strengths and weaknesses of their campaigns. DREAM University started on the second day, and workshops included "Lobbying 101," "The Role of Allies,"

"New Member Orientation," "Know Your Rights in a Police Stop," "Recruiting," and "The Education Not Deportation (END) Campaign."

For me the most important part of the conference started at the beginning of each session, when one or two DREAMers told their stories. Rosa, for example, told us how she taught writing in a small Arkansas high school and how her mentoring of undocumented students led eight of them to attend college in the fall. Elvita described her family's attempts to cross the border and her rape by their guide when she was eleven.

In many ways it was a group therapy session. Here was a safe, protected place where stories could be told, emotions could surface, and a sympathetic and empathetic audience would understand. Their stories shared not only themes of anxiety and depression but also expressions of joy and hope for the future. The DREAMers spoke about not only their challenges but also their choices to live normal lives, learn to deal with insecurity, fight back, and organize to bring about change. It was clear to me that their stories were their most powerful tools.

At the end of the conference, I was asked to speak, and I talked about my book and the power of their stories. I wanted to interview as many of them as possible (and if they were not available for an interview, to get a written biography). I collected almost fifty stories and discovered many of the DREAMers had graduated with honors, made the dean's list, and were class valedictorians. These talented students gave me a glimpse into their lives, and their stories often moved me. I soon discovered a common theme: the consequences of being undocumented. These students and thousands like them live in the shadows and present one self to the world and another to their families and friends.

Most of my subjects lived at home and often had to convince their parents that college was worth it. Parents feared that trips to campus raised the risk of arrest and deportation, and many spoke to their children with a sense of fatalism. For example, one student's parents said, "You get a degree, but you still won't get a real job. You need to work; the family needs the money."

Throughout the book I have highlighted the challenges the undocumented face in pursuit of a higher education. I cannot begin, however, to convey the stress and anxiety these students have endured as a result of their immigration status. During a focus group I discovered that nearly one-third of the group was on medication for anxiety and depression. Seldom do psychological costs enter the conversation on the undocumented—what it is like to live in a state of marginalization, with the fear of arrest and deportation one traffic stop away.

In this chapter I share the insights and experiences of two remarkable young people who have overcome barriers, Juan Mendez and Zessna Garcia. Both have come out as undocumented and are DREAMer activists. Their stories describe the challenges they face and their persistence, determination, and courage.

Juan Mendez

I first met Juan at a meeting organized by University of Arkansas chancellor G. David Gearhart. The Arkansas Department of Higher Education

Juan Mendez, student, business owner, entrepreneur, activist, and DREAMer.
©2012 University Relations. Photograph by Russell Cothren.

had introduced a policy that required Social Security numbers be included on college admissions forms. Chancellor Gearhart recognized that the policy would create a $9,000 increase in tuition for undocumented students, and he assembled campus leaders to discuss how the university could help make higher education accessible and affordable to the growing number of undocumented youth in the state. Juan was one of the attendees. Out of this meeting came a number of strategies and the idea for this book.

The following year, I had several opportunities to watch Juan in action. He was one of the organizers of the District 5 DREAMers United meeting in Fayetteville, Arkansas, a gathering of nearly one hundred representatives from four adjoining states. He also spoke at several other DREAMers events on campus that I attended. I have been impressed with his poise and thoughtful presentations on the DREAM movement to a wide range of audiences. Juan is a handsome and confident young man who has a presence whenever he walks into a room. He is a fearless, passionate, and effective spokesman for the DREAM movement. Fluent in English and Spanish, he effortlessly moves among cultures and groups.

Juan lives in Johnson, Arkansas, a town of 3,500 just north of Fayetteville that is infamous for its speed traps. Juan has lived in Johnson since 2005, where he is well known and liked. He has been an exemplary member of his community, and he knows most of the town's small police force. In June 2012, Juan was driving two undocumented youth to the Mexican consulate in Little Rock to get the documents they needed for their deferred action applications. He stopped at a local station to fill up, and a few minutes later, a Johnson police officer pulled in and said, "Juan, you know your front headlight is out?"

Juan said, "Thanks. I'll take care of it before I get on the interstate."

The officer said, "I'll just give you a warning. Let me see your registration and driver's license." Juan did not, however, have a driver's license.

As he explains the encounter:

> The cop said, "I'm going to have to give you a ticket for the driver's license, but I'll just give you a warning for the headlight. Why don't you have a driver's license?"

I said, "I just never got around to having one. I've always been a business owner, and I haven't had time to go get one."

He said, "That surprises me, Juan. Go get your driver's license."

"I'd been pulled over three times before," Juan continues. "For the first time ever, I wasn't afraid. I felt like I'm tired of being afraid. He is going to do what he's going to do. . . . I'm in a bind. You can't live in northwest Arkansas without a car. The area has a lousy bus system. Cabs are too expensive, and I have a small business. . . . I have to drive to compete for jobs, make deliveries, and do installations."

I interviewed Juan the day before his court appearance, and he was worried. The presiding judge, Ernest Cate, was from Springdale, and his normal penalty for a first offense for driving without a driver's license was two days in jail and a fine. Springdale has a cooperative agreement with ICE, however, which runs background checks on Hispanics while they are in jail. If they are undocumented, an ICE officer rearrests them for deportation upon their release.

The small courtroom was packed. Judge Cate called the court to order and worked through the docket. When Juan's name was called, he walked to the well and pleaded guilty. Then, with his life and livelihood on the line, he began a ten-minute conversation with the judge on the DREAM Act. He was respectful and well spoken and described the plight of DREAMers trying to live and work in Arkansas without a car.

Interestingly, the judge had a brother-in-law who, he said, "arrived in the U.S. in the trunk of a Monte Carlo." In fact, Judge Cate was sponsoring his brother-in-law for citizenship. He said to Juan, "I'm sympathetic to your plight, but the law is clear. You must have a driver's license to drive in Arkansas, and I must enforce the law."

Juan received a $145 fine and two days in jail, suspended. Juan continued to plead the case of the DREAMers, and I thought to myself, "Juan, you got a break. Shut up and get out of here!"

Finally, he said to the judge, "Thank you for listening. Thank you for understanding the problems faced by the undocumented. I'm sorry for all the young people you see without a license, but I think the new deferred action policy is going to help a lot."

Juan extended his hand, and he and Judge Cate shook hands.

Arrival and Early Years

Juan arrived in the United States when he was seven. His family's hometown is two hours south of Presidio, Texas. His parents were married in their late teens, and as Juan describes it, their "economic status wasn't all that bad." His dad had two years of college, but in Mexico "you have to know somebody that knows somebody that knows somebody to be able to get into school and get a scholarship." When his father lost his contact, he had to leave school.

There is a lot of his father in Juan, and he describes him this way:

> I guess you could say my dad always had the entrepreneur in him, and he would always try to get stuff brought from the U.S. over to Mexico, and he would always try to work out deals so that he could resell it at a better price and make a little money here. . . . We tried opening a restaurant, but the corruption and the people that you have to know make it very, very difficult. So if we came here, it's not because we didn't try in Mexico. We tried every single thing in Mexico to try to make money, to try to make a living, but it just wasn't possible.

Juan goes on to describe the violence and corruption in Mexico:

> It's sad to see the violence in Mexico, especially towards business owners. Dad was friends with someone who owned a marketplace, and he was actually killed last year. I guess he wouldn't pay what they were asking him to pay monthly. And so to think that we did not make it back then, and are now here, is a huge blessing, because I think we would be in the same boat that I think a lot of people are in. It is very difficult to own a business and be able to succeed without being targeted by extortion and stuff like that.

It was clear that the family didn't have much of a future in Chihuahua State, Mexico. As I have described earlier, economic opportunity draws the vast majority of immigrants to the United States, and this is borne out in Juan's story and those of the other undocumented youth I interviewed.

Juan's father exemplifies my earlier point that those who emigrate are different from those who stay behind. Moving to another society is fraught with risk, and immigrants who come here for economic opportunities tend to be better educated, more motivated, and entrepreneurial. The bottom line is that immigration is a transfer of human capital from the sending society to our society.

Juan's family arrived in Springdale, Arkansas, on September 17, 1997. Unlike many of the students I interviewed, they were able to cross the border on a tourist visa. Like most immigrants to the United States, they were part of an immigration stream that linked their hometown to a U.S. city. Juan's mother had a sister who lived in Springdale, and his aunt had saved enough money to bring her sister and two other family members across. Either Juan's father or a child would have to stay behind. His mother refused. Juan says, "It was all of us or none of us." Juan's grandmother came to the rescue and pawned her refrigerator to keep the family together. Within a week of arriving in Springdale, Juan's father found a job and sent money home so that his grandmother could reclaim her property.

Earliest Memories and School

Juan's earliest memory of Springdale is of John Tyson Elementary. He notes, "It's a wonderful school, but it's also evidence that Springdale wasn't ready for the Hispanic population explosion at the time." He had a "wonderful teacher," but she "wasn't quite trained to handle someone who didn't speak English. There were three or four of us who didn't speak English. . . . She always put us in a group alone, so we wouldn't slow everybody else down. We had ESL classes, but they were very slow paced. Very slow paced."

Learning English was Juan's passion, and he believes that

> as children, we are sponges, and if I learned English, it was because of my own will and because I had the interest in it. Whatever they gave me in school, I would go home and go over and over and over it. In two days I knew my ABCs, and I was already able to say sentences about going to the restroom and I was hungry— just stuff like that to express myself to the teacher, but it wasn't because the teaching was all that good. It was the interest in, and the need for, a new person in this culture to speak English as soon as possible.

I asked when he became fluent in English. He says, "Maybe three or four months. . . . I had a thick accent at the time, but I was getting better." Today, Juan has a noticeable Arkansas accent.

Self-Deportation and Making a Living

The 2012 presidential campaign was heating up when I interviewed Juan and students like him, and Governor Mitt Romney's position on the undocumented was that they should "self-deport" and reenter the United States legally. I asked Juan about it.

> I think he is out of his mind. A lot of political contributors call him out of touch. He has no idea how the system works. If there were a way to do that, don't you think we would have already done that? Being an undocumented isn't fun. If there was a way for us to just leave the country and apply to return, then of course we'd do it. . . . And Romney only speaks of deportation. I don't think he's actually looked at how many people actually own their own homes and businesses. I would like the banks to step up and say something about this issue. How many banks would be out of business just from people abandoning their homes, businesses, and vehicles?

In a follow-up question, I asked about his network back in his hometown and if he could get a job there. He has a kin network, but he has not seen them since he was a child. With some resignation, he says, "I could probably get a job there. It would be a very low-paying job."

Contrast this with Juan's experience in the United States. He and his family own small businesses that provide jobs, payrolls, and local, state, and federal taxes—they have helped grow our local economy. His take on the Hispanic community's impact on the regional economy is interesting: "We spend; we are spenders; and we are cash spenders. A lot of people don't like to have their money in banks . . . and most of the time we save up and buy it for cash. [As a business owner] it is very good for businesses."

Community and Social Networks

I knew Juan was from a very close-knit family, but I wanted to know more about his friends, neighbors, school, church, and the community he lived in. My research on the region's Hispanic community found that the Catholic Church provided the undocumented with many of the services usually provided by city and state governments. Juan's experiences with the church were, though, not positive. He attended mass but found the nearby church difficult to work with. In 2010, however, he moved to Delaware for a month with two friends and had a much different experience. As he explains it:

> How involved the church was with the community is something that I always wish we had here in Arkansas. The priests were always very involved in whatever we were doing. They volunteered to help with almost any activity we had—if we needed the church office or space for meetings—they were willing to help out with anything we needed.

It was this trip that made him realize the importance of allies—if not the church, then colleges and universities and the business community.

> I had never really had a lot of Mexican or Latino friends until I came to the [University of Arkansas]. At the university I met a lot of people like myself who were undocumented and were just trying to get by and get an education. I found a big support network because they understood what I was going through. I was always afraid of my friends finding out my status because I had a feeling they wouldn't understand why it was I was going through this. So finding other students like myself was a huge relief.

Becoming a DREAMer Activist

Later in our interview, Juan touched on a growing tension that my research uncovered between the DREAMers and the League of United Latin American Citizens (LULAC), the largest and oldest Latino advocacy group in the nation. Juan describes this tension as follows: "I realized that there wasn't really anyone doing anything for the student. We had LULAC, but they were tied down with the higher councils, the national organization. They were really slow about deciding if they wanted to support the DREAM Act, and some of the other organizations in the area were iffy about it too. There was a need."

Juan was one of the founders and one of the core activists in the

DREAM movement in Arkansas. I asked him to tell me about his start with the DREAM movement. The crucial event was a phone call Juan got from a DREAMer organizer who asked him to come to Minnesota for a strategy and training meeting. He says:

> The meeting was awesome. It was like we were in control of the movement. We were no longer dealing with groups putting up boundaries. All my life I've always seen politics as something that I never wanted to be involved with because, like my parents and many other people from Mexico and Latin America, you see politics as something very corrupt, very nasty. . . . But then I was invited [to the training program]. I met the DREAMers that were there trying to build something. They told me that they would be happy to have me on board. I was skeptical at first because of the politics. I remember when I came home, I cried when I saw my parents. On this trip I shared my experience of being undocumented with complete strangers, and I felt very empowered. Yet for the first time I felt vulnerable because I had built this wall around me about being undocumented. . . . I felt vulnerable and I cried.

Juan returned to Arkansas committed and energized, and the first item on his agenda was a DREAM event at the University of Arkansas in February 2010. The local DREAMers planned to hold a rally, take its success back to the community, start working together, and hold another event in April. Unfortunately, the weather was terrible, and rather than the three hundred demonstrators they had expected, a few dozen showed up for the rally. Most of the organizers were crestfallen, but Juan saw it differently. He said, "No, this is awesome because we are taking the step that no one has taken before."

During the District 5 United We Dream conference, many of the DREAM representatives described their efforts to stop anti-immigration bills in their state legislatures. The Arkansas DREAMers faced similar challenges. Juan and his fellow DREAMers attended a session of the Arkansas legislature to block the passage of HB 1008, a bill modeled after Arizona's anti-immigration law. During a break, Juan had a discussion with Jeannie Burlsworth, the founder and chairman of Secure Arkansas, the state's most vocal anti-immigrant organization. Juan's debate with Burlsworth has become legend in the DREAMer community.

As Juan describes the episode:

> So I walked up to her and said, "Ms. Burlsworth, I'm Juan, and I'm a DREAMer."
>
> She said, "Oh, it's very nice to meet you," and she tried to walk away.
>
> But I said, "I was hoping we could talk for a few minutes about this bill."
>
> She said, "Sure."
>
> So we began talking and sat on a bench and talked for a good forty-five minutes. She shared her views, and I told her my story. I let her know I didn't want to cause her harm. I wanted to help Arkansas. I told her in reality we weren't that different. The difference was she had a different approach than I did.
>
> One of her staffers kept trying to get her to leave. She told them we were talking, and we moved to a better location to talk.
>
> At the end of the conversation, I said, "After what I've shared with you, do you think someone like me should be deported?"
>
> She said, "No."
>
> It was something that let me know there is something there. There is power of the story of self for DREAMers. There is a power in our struggle that people need to see. If they realize all we want to do is help and contribute, then their perspective changes.

Within a year, Arkansas DREAMers became an affiliate of DREAMers United, the movement's national umbrella organization. Arkansas DREAMERs were part of the actions that led to the Department of Homeland Security's announcement of deferred action.

Juan is excited about the opportunities to have a driver's license and work permit and to travel within the United States. He is relieved of the daily burden of arrest and deportation. But as a leader of the movement, he has some apprehension. He feels that the DREAMers have a lot to prove.

> It depends on how we treat this opportunity, how we behave. How we use these new opportunities will determine what happens next. . . . DREAMers need to be quick on their feet and do any job that comes up. It's going to be a unique opportunity. We are going to have to represent what our movement is all about because if we're out there, working, putting food on the table,

and more money in our pockets for school and paying bills, I hope that the American people will feel satisfied that they did the right thing. Comprehensive reform is the solution, but it's up to us, the DREAMers who are qualified for deferred action, to prove that one million of us are going to make a positive impact.

Zessna Garcia

I met Zessna through the August 2011 conference and interviewed her twice. I was touched by her story and impressed with her poise and

Zessna Garcia speaking at Undocumented: Living in the Shadows, Fayetteville Town Center, April 23, 2012. More than seven hundred attended the event, where she declared she was "undocumented and unafraid." ©2012 University Relations. Photograph by Russell Cothren.

insights into the undocumented experience. A few weeks after my first interview with Zessna, Chancellor Gearhart asked me to join a planning committee for an upcoming event on the DREAM Act. He was convinced that the university had an important role in encouraging civil, civic debate on the topic. In putting together the program, we chose six state and national DREAMer activists to appear on a panel, and Zessna represented Arkansas. The program, Undocumented: Coming Out of the Shadows, was held in the spring of 2012.[2] More than seven hundred people filled Fayetteville's Town Center, and thousands of others watched it on streaming video.

After the event, I asked Zessna, "What did you think about the evening? Did you think there would be more than seven hundred people who would show up?"

Zessna reflected a moment and said, "I was expecting a much smaller crowd. I never in my wildest dreams expected that many people to come out and listen and show their support for something that is so important, something that affects a lot of us personally." After pausing for a moment, she admitted being nervous, saying, "It was the fact that I was coming out to so many people at one time. I've come out to individuals and small groups, but never seven hundred people."

Arrival and Early Childhood

Zessna's story is common among DREAMers. She arrived in the United States when she was three and settled in Bentonville, Arkansas. Zessna's parents "came for jobs and economic opportunity." Her family had a successful butcher's shop in Gomez Palacio, Durango, Mexico, until her grandfather died. Recalling her parents' story, she says, "No one was able to take care of the shop because everyone was too young. So while this was all happening, everyone started looking for different ways to help out the family. A couple of them moved up north and settled here."

Like Juan's, Zessna's story reflects the experiences of many immigrants: they follow a migration stream that links their hometown with their destination. Today, Zessna has twenty-two cousins and eight aunts and uncles living in the area. She explains, "My parents' original plan was only to be here for a couple of years, raise enough money to pay for their home in Mexico, and go back home and continue their life there. That is the plan that everyone has. Work for a bit, send money back, and go back, but it doesn't happen for most of us."

Zessna's earliest memories are of "moving into a little blue house a couple of blocks from the Bentonville Square. . . . I remember because I lived with my cousins and my aunt and my uncle, and because that was our very first home. After my parents found good, stable jobs, we moved out and lived in a small apartment not far from the Bentonville Square."

Like many of the undocumented I interviewed, Zessna was the only undocumented among her siblings. She recognizes that it affects her family life:

> I have two sisters and a brother. I think it's harder on my sister. All of them were born here, but the oldest of them will be turning eighteen soon. . . . I can't take her to get her driver's license. I don't drive. She has to wait until she's eighteen to apply for certain things because we can't apply for her. So I think she feels it, as well, and it puts a lot of pressure on her, pressure that I don't think she needs to have.

Zessna's Education

Zessna's mother had an English degree, and even before they moved here, she would teach her "English words here and there." Soon after arriving in Arkansas, Zessna was enrolled in a preschool where she was the only Spanish speaker. She says, "[I] learned little bits of English from my mom, learned little bits from my preschool, and I learned it through reading because I love to read." She was fluent within months.

I asked her, "What was your experience in high school like? Were teachers supportive?"

She said yes but paused for a moment and shared, "No one in my high school knew I was undocumented, and since there were so few Hispanics in town, the immigration issue would come up in class from time to time. It was kind of an odd situation to be put in. No one would outwardly come out and say, this is my very strong viewpoint against it. . . . But they were very conservative in their views on immigration policies."

"Did you find that hurtful?" I asked.

"Yes. Flat out yes," she replied.

Zessna found it frustrating that because most of her friends were Anglo, they didn't have a clue to her status. "No one suspected it, because I was really involved with the choir, with the theater program, with volunteering—just having the all-American experience."

The Bentonville High School Choir was invited to sing at Carnegie Hall in New York when Zessna was a junior. "It was <u>the</u> moment. My teachers needed to see our IDs to set up our plane tickets and itinerary for New York. At this point I hadn't come out, and I hadn't told anybody about my situation. My parents thought it was now or never. I had to tell my teacher because we didn't want anything to happen."

Zessna used her high school ID, and she says, "It magically worked. Someone was watching over me at that time. But yeah, I had to go talk to my music teacher. And it was quite possibly the hardest conversation I've ever had to have with anybody."

Working

Zessna's parents have stable jobs, but Zessna has worked in the informal economy most of her life. Babysitting came early, and by fifteen she was cleaning apartments. She still babysits. Recently, she started singing with a band in Fayetteville, and she believes it will provide another source of income. She has also helped her father with his construction over the summer. She quips, "It's common among the undocumented. We're all a jack-of-all-trades."

Self-Deportation

The presidential campaign was heating up the week of our interview, and I asked her about Governor Romney's position that illegal immigrants should self-deport, get in line, and apply legally. I hit a nerve with Zessna:

> The idea is absurd. There is no line to apply. My family doesn't have a history in Mexico. I would not be able to apply easily, because I have no documentation stating that I lived in Mexico. I have to prove that I've been in Mexico for a certain number of

years, so I wouldn't be able to even apply. I have a birth certificate that says I was born in Mexico, but I don't have any other documentation stating that I have been in Mexico for said years. . . . And on top of that, there's a ten-year ban on applying because there's an agreement with the U.S. and Mexico. If the Mexican government finds out that you were in the U.S. illegally and you come back, there's a ten-year ban that you cannot come back into the United States. It's a never-ending cycle.

We actually had this situation before in our family. One of my aunts was born here, and after she graduated high school, she decided to go back to Mexico with my grandmother so she could help her out back home. . . . She went back. She tried working there. She tried applying for things, and because she wasn't in the country for however many years, there was no record of her even existing. So she couldn't apply for anything. It was a bit of a struggle. It was a role reversal for her, and it would be exactly the same for me. My country knows that I exist, because they have my birth certificate. But if I were to go back, there's no record of my existence.

I asked her, "Then you are stateless?"
With resignation she answered, "Yes."

Living in Fear

A common theme in my interviews was the fear of arrest and deportation. It became clear that for most of these undocumented students, right beneath the surface was free-floating anxiety over a traffic stop or an ICE sweep. Zessna describes this fear as follows:

It's on my radar. I do have it in the back of my mind every day, but having been involved in DREAM Act–type activities, we know that as long as we don't break the law—another law, I guess [she laughs]—they can't do much to us. So as long as I live a pretty safe, not-too-rowdy life, I can be okay without having that fear of having someone come knocking on my door.

But it's always there. You have to be careful whenever you go out. . . . Just really being careful and trying not to drive without a license, trying not to break the laws, not doing anything small . . . so you won't get a police officer to look at you or question your status.

College Experiences

Zessna always knew she was going to go college, but she did not know how she was going to get there. She was in one of the top choirs in the state, and her teachers told her she was almost guaranteed a scholarship. She applied to several schools in the region, but as soon as they learned that she did not have a social security number, they stopped her application.

Even with these obstacles, Zessna has earned an associate's degree from Northwest Arkansas Community College, and she now is a University of Arkansas student. She pays nonresident tuition, however, which doubles the cost, and she takes only one course a semester, which is what her family can afford. She says, "The DREAM Act would take a huge load off of my family because it would end my out-of-state tuition. The family budget is based on my tuition, and that limits us a lot—not only for me but for my siblings, as well. It's a lot of what they can and can't do and what our family is able to do together."

DREAMers

"Before I got involved with the DREAM Act, I didn't really speak about it," says Zessna. "I didn't speak about my status. It wasn't something that I ever wanted to talk about."

Her activism began four years ago during a meeting in Conway, Arkansas, organized by Juan Mendez and several other activists. Zessna says, "I knew that I needed to get involved if something were to happen. I wanted to be there firsthand to know and not to hear it from someone else. [After the meeting] I started talking to students at the high school level and worked with Juan and the Arkansas DREAMers. Then, in May of that same year, Juan and one of his friends traveled to Delaware to help kick start the movement there." She joined them.

Zessna spent the summer talking to congressmen and community organizers and helping to set up a Delaware DREAM team. "We were there for a little less than a month, and we were able to set this all up, and we left the state in pretty good hands." Later, after a meeting in Washington with the national coordinator of United We Dream, the Arkansas group became an affiliate.

A few days before our interview, Director of Homeland Security

Janet Napolitano announced the agency's new policy of deferred action. I asked Zessna, "What does the policy change mean to you? Does it give you a broader outlook on the future?"

Beaming, she said, "Oh, yes. Before deferred action, I was approached by quite a few people giving me an opportunity to do internships or jobs, but I had to decline because I was not able to take them. [With a deferred action] permit, I can contact those people and hopefully get a job." But like many DREAMers, she is concerned that without a federal DREAM Act there is no path to citizenship.

I shared with Zessna some national data on the relatively small impact of the DREAM Act on the 2.1 million undocumented youth in the United States, including the fact that relatively few of those eligible for resident tuition in states like Texas and California take advantage of it. I asked her, "In your mind, why is it important to pass the DREAM Act?" She replied:

> It is very important because it's a stepping stone in the right direction, legalizing a much larger number of undocumented students because you can't have thousands of people working without benefitting from their labor. The important thing is that it could lead to a much larger bill for our family members and others left out of the DREAM Act loop.

We finished the interview by talking about the DREAM movement, the rule of small victories, and the remarkable events of the past few months that had led to the change in DHS policy. Reflecting on her role in this victory, Zessna said, "I'm extremely humbled to have been a part of such a huge movement. Today, we can start sending in our applications for deferred action. It brings such hope to undocumented students."

Final Thoughts

In my research I found that undocumented students were not homogeneous. These students came from diverse ethnic, cultural, and economic backgrounds. Although the majority of the students I interviewed were Hispanic, in my sample were students from Ghana, South Korea, Vietnam, and China. Their biographies reveal diverse backgrounds but common themes—much like those of Juan and Zessna. They arrived here at a young age, and their parents came seeking economic opportunity. Their parents were more motivated, more entrepreneurial, and better educated than the people they left behind. Like the millions of immigrants before them, they followed a migration stream between their hometown and the United States because family members who already lived here lowered the risks of immigration and softened the transition to a new culture, society, and language.

Juan and Zessna, like most of the undocumented youth I interviewed, quickly learned English, benefited from the educational experiences guaranteed in the *Plyler v. Doe* ruling, and have thrived in this society. They volunteer and give back to their communities. Their activism has emerged from their fears of living in the shadows and, after discovering in DREAMer meetings that they were not alone, from others' common experiences.

Juan and Zessna have come out as undocumented and unafraid, knowing full well that this act of defiance and bravery could lead to their arrests and deportation. If you were to meet them, you would not know they were undocumented. They are American in every way except their immigration status. If you were asked, as was anti-immigration leader Jeannie Burlsworth, whether they should be deported, your answer would be a resounding no.

Zessna and Juan represent the best of Generation 1.5. They are bright, intelligent, poised, and articulate. They are struggling to finish their educations under difficult circumstances, but I have no doubt that they will finish. They are a vital part of this nation's human capital, a resource that we should not squander. They and the other DREAMers remind us that we are a nation of immigrants. They are the newest chapter in a process that has created and shaped this nation.

EIGHT

Next Steps
Where We Go from Here

That dream of a land in which life should be better
and richer and fuller for every man, with opportunity
for each according to his ability or achievement. . . .
That dream or hope has been present from the start.

—JAMES TRUSLOW ADAMS, *EPIC OF AMERICA* (1931)

In the first five chapters I addressed the following five most common arguments against the DREAM Act: (1) undocumented students are criminals; (2) passing the DREAM Act would reward and increase illegal immigration; (3) the undocumented burden services and drain tax revenues; (4) immigrants are changing the national character; and (5) immigrants will never assimilate.

As I have shown, the critics have gotten it wrong. We don't hold undocumented children accountable for the behavior of their parents. The undocumented do not come to this country for educational benefits but for economic opportunities, and they pay more in taxes than they consume in services. Our fourth wave immigrants add more than $1 trillion in buying power to our economy. They embrace our values. They are upwardly mobile. They are learning English faster than did previous waves. They are rapidly assimilating and blending into our melting pot nation. And they are coming to this country for the same reasons as past generations—for freedom, liberty, and a better life. Simply, we are repeating the process that built this nation. As in previous waves, we benefit because we need their education, skills, entrepreneurship, and manpower to grow our economy and tax base.

As I show in Chapter 6, the goals of the DREAM Act are modest.

The proposed law would extend the benefits of K–12 education through college by making college more affordable. If undocumented youth completed two years of college or military service over a six-year period and if they exhibited good moral character, they would be granted permanent residency and the opportunity for citizenship. Only 38 percent of the 2.1 million children and youth eligible for the DREAM Act would likely use the benefits. More importantly, the impact of the DREAM Act on state higher education budgets would be negligible.

In chapter 7, I introduce two remarkable DREAMers, Juan and Zessna. When you know their stories, you have to wonder why we would think about deporting them. Don't we want these remarkable young people to be part of our communities and citizens of our nation?

The time is right for the passage of the DREAM Act. The 2012 presidential election has changed the political landscape. The historic turnout by Hispanic voters, driven by the anti-immigration rhetoric of the election, has left the Republican Party soul-searching and many immigrant voters with a greater sense of political voice. In the days following the election, Republican leaders, like Senator Lindsey Graham of South Carolina, have said that the party must change and either welcome our newest immigrants or become irrelevant on the national political stage. Their views are aligning with the growing sentiment that denying these young people an education is not right, and the time has come for Congress to pass the DREAM Act and comprehensive immigration reform. And it is time for those committed to immigration reform to help frame the debate.

Recently, Steve Jobs's widow, Laurene Powell Jobs, said, "We think Congress's inaction . . . is devastating for these students and tragic for the country." She and a group of Silicon Valley technology leaders recently founded Educators for Fair Consideration, a nonprofit that gives scholarships, career advice, and legal services to undocumented youth. Most Americans agree with her.[1] A 2012 Gallup poll reported that 66 percent of Americans thought immigration was a good thing and support was across political parties.[2] And a July 2012 survey of likely voters by Bloomberg reported that 64 percent agreed with President Obama's policy of deferred action.[3] Perhaps, it is time for our politicians to stop listening to a vocal minority, to begin to address the immigration reform that the majority of Americans support, and to do what is right: allow undocumented children and young adults to stay in this country, permit them to go to school and work, provide them with a path to citizenship, and give them the opportunity to contribute to our society. How do we make this happen? How do we get a deeply divided and partisan Congress to do what is good for the nation? I believe the answer lies in our past.

On Thursday, December 1, 1955, an African American woman in Montgomery, Alabama, climbed onto a bus after a ten-hour work day as a seamstress at a local department store.[4] The bus was crowded, and she sat in one of the last seats reserved for blacks. Her seat was in the row immediately behind the white section, but the bus driver noticed a white man standing and told her to stand at the back of the bus. She refused. The driver stopped the bus and called the police, and she was arrested. Rosa Parks's act of courage launched the modern civil rights movement.[5]

The goal of a social movement is to change society. And our democratic experiment has experienced many great movements— revolutionary, abolitionist, suffrage, antiwar, feminist, and gay rights. All social movements have similar elements. They build on what sociologists call strong social ties—family, kin, and friends—and weak social ties—neighbors, coworkers, church members, friends of friends, and community groups. Movements succeed when events create a social climate ripe for change and leaders seize these important historical moments to create a shared vision, a sense of identity, and a common ownership of the movement. For the civil rights movement, the change began in 1955 when the Supreme Court ruled in *Brown v. Board of Education* that school segregation was illegal. The movement gained momentum with the emergence of new leaders like Martin Luther King, Jr. and organizations like the Southern Christian Leadership Conference. All that was needed was a spark, and it was Rosa Parks.

The white leadership of Montgomery, Alabama, could not have arrested a worse person. Montgomery was one of the most networked cities in the nation. In the 1950s whites and blacks belonged to a rich array of church, fraternal, neighborhood, and civic groups. Montgomery's *Directory of Civil and Social Organizations* was as thick as a phone book. Rosa's job as a seamstress brought her into contact with people across social strata, and she was liked and respected by all, from black laborers to white lawyers. Through church and volunteer work, she had built a social network that bridged Montgomery's racial divide. When Parks's friends and family learned of her arrest, her strong ties kicked in—they bailed her out and hired a lawyer. And when word spread through her friends of friends, coworkers, and church and club members, her network of weak ties kicked in, and the black community was mobilized.

Five days after her arrest, a local court found Rosa Parks guilty of violating the city's bus ordinance. More than five hundred blacks gathered outside the courthouse for a peaceful demonstration—the largest in Montgomery's history. Through the leadership of King and others, the idea of a boycott spread through churches and the black press, and the following week, thousands of Montgomery's black residents stayed off the buses. The stage was set for the final ingredient of a social movement—peer pressure, the sense of obligation that neighbors have toward each other in a crisis. Although the boycott wavered at times, it endured, and in a little over a year, her lawsuit worked its way through the courts. On December 17, 1956, the U.S. Supreme Court ruled that Montgomery's bus segregation law was unconstitutional. The following morning, for the first time in over a year, King and his leadership boarded a city bus and sat in front. In the ensuing years, the small victory in Montgomery spread to Selma, Greensboro, Little Rock, and finally Washington, D.C., and in less than a decade, the Congress passed and President Lyndon Johnson signed the Civil Rights Act of 1964 and the Voting Rights Act of 1965. Strong and weak ties, peer pressure, and small victories play a role in all successful social movements.

The civil rights movement gave people outside the mainstream an opportunity to have their voices heard. Lacking power and money and living in communities like Montgomery where racism closed the political process, the black community used its churches and civic organizations as a forum to talk among themselves. Talking led to the belief that the problem would not exist if political and civic leaders had done what they were supposed to do, and over time a shared view of injustice emerged. The arrest of Rosa Parks was the precipitating event: leaders emerged to organize and to provide a sense of direction, and in the next decade the nation was changed forever.

The DREAM movement has a similar history and employs the same organizational principles and philosophy of nonviolence. Long before the passage of anti-immigration laws in Arizona, Alabama, Florida, and Georgia, a feeling of injustice was growing among undocumented youth. Tactics of ICE agents; the Safe Communities Program, which partnered local law enforcement agencies with ICE; the rise in deportations to nearly 400,000 per year; and the growing anti-immigration climate in many communities forced undocumented youth deeper into the shadows. Living in a climate of fear and uncertainty, many began to look outward to others with similar experiences. A common theme among the youth I interviewed was, "I did nothing wrong. I was brought here. I did not come here. I'm an American in every way except my status." To me one of the most fascinating things about the DREAMers has been their use of the Internet and social media to create a unified and mobilized movement. Often isolated in their homes, neighborhoods, and schools, it wasn't just the church or organizations that brought them together but Twitter, IM, e-mail, and the Internet. The first five chapters of this book expose the many challenges endured by undocumented youth, but what is perhaps equally amazing and, certainly, more inspiring is that a group of young people without access to the ballot box could talk, text, and use social media to make known the power of their stories and the justness of their cause. Emerging from the shadows, they have started what the Congress could not—the process of changing federal immigration policy. The United We Dream Network is a textbook example of how personal concerns can be transformed into a social problem that demands government action, and it says much about our democracy.

The United We Dream Network (unitedwedream.org) began in 2009 when ten local DREAM organizations combined under an umbrella organization to develop a national strategy. Today, the organization has thirty-six affiliates in twenty-two states. Recent success has been the result of years of organizing, training, preparing for nonviolent protests, strategic planning, and executing based on the rule of small victories. Many of the network's approaches are taken from the pages of the civil rights movement.[6]

In his 2008 campaign, President Obama promised to pass the DREAM Act if elected. As with *Brown v. Board of Education* a half-century earlier, a sympathetic president in office means we are in a unique place and time to pass the DREAM Act. One of We Dream's first and most effective strategies was the Undocumented and Unafraid campaign, in which undocumented youth who had previously lived their lives in the shadows began to "out" themselves. The DREAMers' outing activity—undocumented youth risking arrest in nonviolent civil disobedience—harkened back to the sit-ins, the desegregations of lunch counters, and the marches of the civil rights era. But in some ways the DREAMers' disobedience was even more courageous because with arrest loomed deportation. A venomous opposition tried to frame the debate around this point, claiming that undocumented youth were foreign, illegal, and threatening. The campaign put a human face to the undocumented, however, and the public saw these young people as Americans in every way except their immigration status.

A second strategy was unveiled when five DREAMers were arrested during a sit-in at Senator John McCain's Tucson office. Paulina Gonzalez, arrested earlier in a nonviolent protest of Arizona's anti-immigration act SB 1070, was there during the planning leading up to the event and describes the groundbreaking organization campaign that followed:

> To maintain message, action, and strategic discipline, locally based DREAM teams led trainings in nonviolence and organizing. Students engaged in campaign research, community based educational events, campus organizing, media outreach, coalition building, social networking, hunger strikes, sit-ins, lobbying visits to the Capitol, and much more. All of it a part of a strategy to generate momentum in support of the idea that young people living in this country without legal documentation had a right to stay and live in this country legally. . . . Weaved into each action, press event, and organizing one-on-ones, movement organizers told both their personal stories, the story of the movement, and made their pitch to action. In this way, the DREAM movement consciously chose to change the frame in which it was organizing.[7]

Building coalitions was part of this strategy, and in March 2010 the AFL-CIO, the American Federation of Teachers, and the National Education Association joined a growing number of organizations supporting passage of the DREAM Act.

We Dream also used dilemma actions, strategically planned events that placed government officials and politicians in a dilemma in which any response advanced the movement's goals. For example, small, nonviolent actions were staged in which undocumented students peacefully submitted to arrest. Cuffed by police, they were led off in graduation caps and gowns, and these images went viral across the social and the mainstream media. Support for the movement grew. Paulina Gonzalez writes, "With these carefully crafted actions, the DREAM Movement presented the Obama Administration and targeted legislators with a dilemma. They forced their targets to make a choice to either arrest and deport college students or support the DREAM Act." None of the arrested were deported.

In the ensuing months, sit-ins were conducted in key legislators' offices across the country. Twenty DREAMers were arrested during sit-ins at the offices of several senators, and a teach-in was held outside the White House. In December 2010 the movement experienced a small victory: the House passed the DREAM Act. Disappointment followed when the bill fell five votes short of cloture in the Senate. Although the bill was filibustered within a year, the rule of small victories would prevail.

Faced with a bitterly divided and partisan Congress, DREAM organizers decided to bypass Congress and pressure the president, demanding that he fulfill his campaign promise. The new goal was not legislation but an executive order that would grant administrative relief to young people living in the country illegally. Thus, the Right to Dream Campaign was born, with the goal of halting the deportation of undocumented youth and granting them the right to work. But was an executive order legal? The answer was yes, and it came in a brief crafted by a team of volunteer attorneys. In October 2011, armed with the legal opinion, a group of DREAMers led a dilemma action at ICE's Los Angeles office. Soon, a memo outlining the DREAMers' demand for administrative relief and presenting their legal argument was delivered to ICE director John T. Morton. A critical paragraph in the memo reads:

> [United We Dream's attorneys] believe, as do many immigration attorneys—that the same power that you exercised in reinvigorating "prosecutorial discretion" can be exercised by the administration in the form of an "application" for administrative

relief. This includes the executive branch's authority—and responsibility—to make decisions on how it will interpret and implement existing law.[8]

The memo went on to argue that the Obama administration had the legal authority to grant DREAMers work permits and to ban students from being put into removal proceedings. At the same time, a letter supporting this opinion was circulating and eventually signed by over ninety immigration law experts from universities around the country.

DREAM movement organizers escalated the Right to Dream Campaign by holding small actions at Obama campaign headquarters. Organizers had met with White House staffers before, but during a critical 2012 meeting, they notified the White House that if the movement had not heard from the administration by June 12, there would be a national week of action in Obama campaign headquarters in swing states like Nevada, Florida, and Colorado.

Lobbying and political action continued, and just two days after the sit-ins began, the Obama administration's Department of Homeland Security issued its deferred action policy. Although not an executive order, it had the same effect, and it met the demands laid out by the Right to Dream Campaign. The issuance of the new DHS policy was a move that surprised even movement organizers.

The victory was years in the making and demonstrated how a well-organized group—diligent in their strategic planning, training, organizing, consensus building, adapting to political change, and executing action—could succeed. The Right to Dream Campaign's determination, discipline, and political will reflect the best of our democracy, the effectiveness of nonviolence, and the importance of accumulating small victories on the road to comprehensive immigration reform. Looking to the future, organizer Carlos Amador sums it up well: "With this victory there is great hope that a larger victory, like comprehensive immigration reform or the DREAM Act, is possible. This is just the beginning; this is the proof that we are going to be able to win something bigger soon."

One of the architects of the civil rights movement, Reverend James Lawson, recently said, "Power comes from ordinary people." And ordinary people can do remarkable things when they organize, plan, and have the courage to act on their convictions. The DREAMers are ordinary people who carefully studied the lessons of the civil rights movement and other nonviolent struggles, and the product of their work was the change in Obama's immigration policy, a first step toward comprehensive immigration reform.

People ask, "Why waste the time, money, and energy working to pass a state DREAM Act?" They say that even if it passes, it's not going to help very many young people. The answer is that it is the right and moral thing to do. It is good for our economy and the nation's future. The way there is paved with small victories, and you can be a part of the next one.

Although I focus for the most part on national campaigns, all politics really are local, and the same steps that led to the success of the civil rights movement and, more recently, the Dream movement are daily playing out at the state and local levels. We need a second front to help pass a national DREAM Act, and this front will be rooted in the states. In twelve states, legislators fed up with a divided, partisan, and unresponsive Congress have taken matters in their own hands and passed their own DREAM Acts. When combined, these laws allow 65 percent of our nation's undocumented youth access to in-state tuition rates, and in California, New York, and Texas, students have access to state-funded financial aid, as well. The state DREAM Acts do not, however, provide permanent residency or paths to citizenship. We need a federal law. More importantly, the DREAM Act doesn't help the more than one million undocumented youth for whom college is out of reach because of language, family, and financial barriers.

There are four sources of political power—money, people, information, and relationships. Money is the lifeblood of all movements, so open your checkbooks and use your credit cards. For a District 5 United We Dream meeting I attended, more than one hundred representatives from Texas, Oklahoma, Kansas, Missouri, and Arkansas converged upon the University of Arkansas campus for a weekend of workshops and planning meetings. There was a little help with gas money. The food was donated by local restaurants, and the out-of-state participants stayed with local supporters or doubled up in motels. The organization does a lot with a little and uses its funds wisely and well. The United We Dream website is at unitedwedream.org;

click the button at the top right to donate to your local United We Dream affiliate.

Power comes from ordinary people, and each of you has a social network that you can tap for support. Faith-based organizations have vast potential because they hold a reservoir of people whose beliefs are based in compassion and caring for others. They also are a constituency that votes. Chambers of commerce, economic development organizations, and companies that want the business of growing immigrant communities are other sources of support. Don't forget the power of social media, and spread the message through your network.

Stay local and build relationships with your elected representatives because a small percentage of the electorate wins elections. Elected officials respond to issue voters because they vote. Find your state representatives at www.ncsl.org/about-us/ncslservice/state-legislative-websites-directory.aspx and your U.S. senators and congresswomen and congressmen at congress.org/congressorg/directory/congdir.tt.

You've read the book, so now you can frame the issue based on the facts that we are a nation of immigrants, that we are continuing a process that has made us great, that this process grows our economy and expands our tax base, and that the DREAM Act would allow young people who we have already educated from K–12 to become college graduates and make a lifelong contribution to our society. Counter myths and misinformation. Keep your message straightforward, direct, and consistent, and share with others the progress of legislation in your states. Put a face to the DREAM movement, and meet a DREAMer. Listen to his or her story. Build relationships by telling and retelling their stories, and help them expand their network of relationships, which, in turn, will help them build alliances.

Ordinary people can do extraordinary things, and social movements often succeed along a path of small victories. I hope this book has shown you that we have nothing to fear from our newest wave of immigrants. We are repeating a process that has created this nation and made it strong. I hope you appreciate that undocumented youth have done nothing wrong and are being unfairly punished for the behavior of their parents. I hope you agree that this nation has everything to gain and little to lose in giving the best and brightest of the 2.1 million undocumented youth access to higher education, better jobs, bigger paychecks, and larger contributions to our tax base. I hope you appreciate how important these young people are to our labor force, military, and the future of Medicare and Social Security. And I hope you will join a growing number of Americans who feel that the inaction of our Congress is wrong and devastating to these young people. Please join us in passing your state's DREAM Act. Join the fourteen states that have sent the message to Congress that if they can't do their job, we will. Taking the legislative initiative will demonstrate the power of our democracy and make a better and more prosperous America for us all.

NOTES

ANSWERING THE CRITICS

1. On November 19, 2012, Massachusetts Governor Deval Patrick directed state colleges and universities to allow young undocumented immigrants to pay in-state tuition as soon as they obtained work permits through Homeland Security's Deferred Action for Childhood Arrivals policy.

2. In June 2001, Texas (HB 1403) was the first state to pass legislation allowing in-state tuition for immigrant students, followed by California (AB 540), Utah (HB 144), and New York (SB 7784) in 2001–2; Washington (HB 1079), Oklahoma (SB 596) and Illinois (HB 60) in 2003; Kansas (HB 2145) in 2004; New Mexico (SB 582) in 2005; Nebraska (LB 239) in 2006; Wisconsin (A 75) in 2009; and Maryland (S 167/H 470) and Connecticut (H 6390) in 2011. In September 2011, Rhode Island's Board of Governors for Higher Education approved policy to allow unauthorized students to pay in-state tuition at public colleges. Wisconsin rescinded their law in 2011, however, with bill A40.

1. THESE CHILDREN ARE BLAMELESS

1. For excellent histories and overviews of the nation's immigration laws, see Marc Rosenblum, *U.S. Immigration Policy since 9/11: Understanding the Stalemate over Comprehensive Immigration Reform* (Washington, D.C.: Migration Policy Institute, 2011); Katie Annand, "Still Waiting for the Dream: The Injustice of Punishing Undocumented Immigrant Students," *Hasting College of Law Journal* 59, no. 3 (2008): 683–710. Rosenblum describes the criminalization of immigration in the post-9/11 era and the factors that have contributed to the legislative stalemate in Washington. Annand focuses on the DREAM Act and analyzes the criminalization of immigration, the current law surrounding undocumented youth and education, the provisions and legislative history of the act, and why theories of criminal punishment do not apply to undocumented youth.

2. Jennifer L. Maki, "The Three R's: Reading, Riting, and Rewarding Illegal Immigrants: How Higher Education Has Acquiesced in the Illegal Presence of Undocumented Aliens in the United States," *William & Mary Bill of Rights Journal* 13 (2005): 1340–73. Maki's article provides a summary of the opponents' positions on the DREAM Act.

3. For a recording of the oral arguments in *Plyler v. Doe*, along with the transcript and Justice Brennan's opinion for the majority (457 U.S 202 [1982]), see "Plyler v. Doe," Oyez Project at IIT Chicago-Kent College of Law website, last updated December 18, 2012, www.oyez.org/cases/1980-1989/1981/1981_80_1538.

4. Damien Cave, "For Mexicans Looking North, a New Calculus Favors Home," *New York Times* website, July 6, 2011, www.nytimes.com/interactive/2011/07/06/world/americas/immigration.html.

5. These interviews took place at the United We Dream workshop at the University of Arkansas, August 12–14, 2011, and in my office that fall. Given the undocumented status of most of the students I interviewed, I have changed their names to protect their identities. Rocio's interviews were conducted by e-mail. She also provided an autobiography.

6. Cave, "For Mexicans Looking North."

7. See Cave, "For Mexicans Looking North"; Jeffrey Passel and D'Vera Cohn, *Unauthorized Immigrant Population: National and State Trends, 2010* (Washington, D.C.: Pew Research Center, 2011); Mark H. Lopez, Ana Gonzalez-Barrera, and Seth Motel, *As Deportations Rise to Record Levels, Most Latinos Oppose Obama Policy* (Washington, D.C.: Pew Hispanic Center, 2011).

8. This section follows the legal theories upon which the DREAM Act is based, as described in Annand, "Still Waiting for the Dream."

9. U.S. Census Bureau, "Current Population Survey: Annual Social and Economic Supplement," U.S. Census Bureau website, last updated September 13, 2011, www.census.gov/hhes/www/cpstables/032011/perinc/new03_028.htm.

10. For the University of Arkansas's tuition costs for the 2012–13 academic year, see "Financial Affairs: Treasurer's Office: Tuition and Fees Information," University of Arkansas website, treasurer.uark.edu/Tuition.asp?pagestate=Average.

2. IMMIGRATION 101

1. Joseph M. Cervantes, Olga L. Mejia, and Amalia Guerrero Mena, "Serial Migration and the Assessment of 'Extreme and Unusual Psychological Hardship' with Undocumented Latina/o Families," *Hispanic Journal of Behavioral Sciences* 32, no. 2 (2010): 275–91.

2. Roberto G. Gonzales, "Wasted Talent and Broken Dreams: The Lost Potential of Undocumented Students," *Focus: Immigration Policy* 5, no. 3 (2007): 12.

3. Donald M. Kerwin, Doris Meissner, and Margie McHugh, *Executive Action on Immigration: Six Ways to Make the System Work Better* (Washington, D.C.: Migration Policy Institute, 2011).

3. SPEND A TRILLION DOLLARS A YEAR AND YOU ARE A TAX BURDEN?

1. This paragraph is based on summaries of interviews provided on the ABC News and Fox News websites and a report on immigration cost posted on the FAIR website. Ed Barnes, "Illegal Immigration Costs U.S. $113 Billion a Year, Study Finds," Fox News website, July 6, 2010, http://www.foxnews.com/us/2010/07/02/immigration-costs-fair-amnesty-educations-costs-reform; Dalia Fahmy, "Expensive Aliens: How Much Do Illegal Immigrants Really Cost?," ABC News website, May 21, 2010, http://abcnews.go.com/Business/illegal-immigrants-cost-us-100-billion-year-group/story?id=10699317#.T5HPMe2TR1M; Federation for American Immigration Reform, "The Fiscal Burden of Illegal Immigration on U.S. Taxpayers," FAIR website, July 2010, revised February 2011, http://www.fairus.org/site/DocServer/USCostStudy_2010.pdf?docID=4921.

2. Ernesto Zedillo, "Migranomics Instead of Walls, " *Forbes,* January 2007, 25–26.

3. Eduardo Porter, "Illegal Immigrants Are Bolstering Social Security with Billions," *New York Times,* April 5, 2005.

4. Immigration Policy Center, "Unauthorized Immigrants Pay Taxes, Too," Immigration Policy Center website, April 18, 2011, http://immigrationpolicy.org/just-facts/unauthorized-immigrants-pay-taxes-too.

5. Oregon Center for Public Policy, *Undocumented Workers Are Taxpayers, Too* (Silverton, OR: Oregon Center for Public Policy, 2012).

6. Randy Capps, Everett Henderson, John D. Kasarda Jr., James H. Johnson, Stephen J. Appold, Derrek L. Croney, Donald J. Hernandez, and Michael Fix, *A Profile of Immigrants in Arkansas* (Washington, D.C.: Urban Institute, 2007).

7. Barnes, "Illegal Immigration Costs U.S. $113 Billion a Year."

8. Jeffrey S. Passel, *Net Migration from Mexico Falls to Zero—and Perhaps Less* (Washington, D.C.: Pew Hispanic Center, 2012).

9. M. J. Piore finds that many industrial societies attract migrant laborers because the native-born workforce is unwilling to stay in bottom-level jobs. He also finds that migrant workers are willing to work in positions that increase their relative economic standing in their native communities. M. J. Piore, *Birds of Passage: Migrant Labor in Industrial Societies* (Cambridge: Cambridge University Press, 1979).

10. George J. Borjas, *Measuring the Impact on Native-Born Workers* (Washington, D.C.: Center for Immigration Studies, 2004).

11. Gordon H. Hanson, *The Economics and Policy of Illegal Immigration in the United States* (Washington, D.C.: Migration Policy Institute, 2009).

12. Read the provisions of Arizona's SB 1070, Support Our Law Enforcement and Safe Neighborhoods Act, at http://www.azleg.gov/legtext/49leg/2r/bills/sb1070h.pdf.

13. Raúl Hinojosa-Ojeda and Marshall Fitz, *A Rising Tide or a Shrinking Pie: The Economic Impact of Legalization versus Deportation in Arizona* (Washington, D.C.: Center for American Progress Immigration Policy Center, 2011).

14. Daniel González, "Arizona's Immigration Population Plunges" *Arizona Republic,* March 23, 2012, http://www.azcentral.com/arizonarepublic/news/articles/20120323arizona-illegal-migrant-population-plunges.html.

15. Hinojosa-Ojeda and Fitz, *A Rising Tide or a Shrinking Pie.*

16. For a summary of the Alabama Immigration Law (Act No. 2011-535), see the State of Alabama Office of the Attorney General website at http://www.ago.alabama.gov/Page-Immigration-Act-No-2011-535-Text.

17. Samuel Addy, *A Cost-Benefit Analysis of the New Alabama Immigration Law* (Tuscaloosa: University of Alabama, 2012).

18. Gustavo Valdes and Catherine E. Shoichet, "Auto Exec's Arrest a New Flashpoint in Alabama's Immigration Debate," CNN website, November 22, 2011, http://articles.cnn.com/2011-11-22/us/us_alabama-immigration-arrest_1_immigration-law-check-immigration-status-immigration-debate?_s=PM:US; Ed Pilkington, "Alabama Red-Faced as Second Foreign Car Boss Held under Immigration Law," *Guardian* website, December 2, 2011, http://www.guardian.co.uk/world/2011/dec/02/alabama-car-boss-immigration-law.

19. Ed Pilkington, "Alabama Immigration: Crops Rot as Workers Vanish to Avoid Crackdown," *Guardian* website, October 14, 2011, http://www.guardian.co.uk/world/2011/oct/14/alabama-immigration-law-workers.

20. Pilkington, "Alabama Immigration."

21. R. J. Epstein, "Hispanics Flee from New Alabama Immigration Law," *Politico* website, June 29, 2011, http://www.politico.com/news/stories/0611/58049.html.

22. Roy L. Williams, "Alabama Immigration Law Blamed for Drop in Construction Jobs," November 30, 2011, http://blog.al.com/businessnews/2011/11/alabama _immigration_law_blamed.html.

23. Addy, *A Cost-Benefit Analysis,* 9.

24. K. Belson and J. P. Capuzzo, "Town Rethink Laws against Illegal Immigrants," *New York Times* website, September 26, 2007, http://www.nytimes.com/2007/09/26/nyregion/26riverside.html?_r=1&pagewanted=all.

25. Reuters, "Supreme Court Splits Its Verdict on Arizona Immigration Law," Reuters website, June 26, 2012, http://www.reuters.com/article/2012/06/26/us-usa-immigration-court-idUSBRE85O0Q520120626.

26. Sam Fahmy, "Despite Recession, Hispanic and Asian Buying Power Expected to Surge in U.S., According to Annual UGA Selig Center Multicultural Economy Study," University of Georgia website, November 4, 2010, http://www.terry.uga.edu/news/releases/2010/minority-buying-power-report.html.

27. Fahmy, "Despite Recession."

28. Immigration Policy Center, "The New Americans in Arkansas: The Political and Economic Power of Immigrants, Latinos, and Asians in the Natural State," Immigration Policy Center website, January 2012, http://www.immigrationpolicy.org/sites/default/files/docs/New_Americans_in_Arkansas_2012_0.pdf.

29. Raúl Hinojosa-Ojeda and Paule C. Takash, *No Dreamers Left Behind: The Economic Potential of Dream Act Beneficiaries* (Los Angeles: North American Integration and Development Center, 2011).

4. SALSA, AMERICA'S NUMBER-ONE CONDIMENT

1. U.S. Department of Homeland Security, Office of Immigration Statistics, *2010 Yearbook of Immigration Statistics* (Washington, D.C.: Government Printing Office, 2011), Table 3.

2. U.S. Census Bureau, "Most Children Younger than Age 1 Are Minorities," U.S. Census Bureau website, May 17, 2012, http://www.census.gov/newsroom/releases/archives/population/cb12-90.html.

3. Nathan P. Walters and Edward Trevelyan, "The Newly Arrived Foreign-Born Population of the United States: 2010," U.S. Census Bureau website, November 2011, http://www.census.gov/prod/2011pubs/acsbr10-16.pdf.

4. Philip Martin and Elizabeth Midgley, *Immigration: Shaping and Reshaping America* (Washington, D.C.: Population Reference Bureau, 2003).

5. Federation for American Immigration Reform, "About FAIR," FAIR website, http://www.fairus.org/about.

6. Cato Institute, "Immigration Fact and Fiction," Cato Institute website, July 1, 2010, http://www.cato.org/multimedia/daily-podcast/immigration-fact-fiction.

7. Mass immigration is thought to be a major factor behind the rise of the radical right, but the relationship is not as straightforward as many researchers would suggest. Cas Mudde explores this relationship with data from North America and

western, central, and eastern Europe. One of few clear findings is that the radical right (regardless of nation) frames the immigration debate along two major themes—a cultural threat (attack on common cultural and religious values and an unwillingness of immigrant groups to assimilate) and a security threat (crime and terrorism). In recent years the governments of the United States and most industrialized nations have tightened immigration policies, but the political right, operating outside the mainstream political parties, has been only one of many factors responsible for this policy change. There are also important countervailing pressures, like the enforcement of existing antidiscrimination laws and powerful pro-immigrant political groups. See Cas Mudde, *The Relationship between Immigration and Nativism in Europe and North America* (Washington, D.C.: Migration Policy Institute, 2012).

8. Mudde, *The Relationship between Immigration and Nativism.*

9. Peter Schrag, *Not Fit for Our Society: Immigration and Nativism in America* (Berkeley: University of California Press, 2011).

10. Hanson, *The Economics and Policy of Illegal Immigration.*

11. Partnership for a New American Economy, "The 'New American' Fortune 500," Partnership for a New American Economy website, June 2011, http://www .renewoureconomy.org/sites/all/themes/pnae/img/new-american-fortune-500 -june-2011.pdf.

12. Evin Rodkey, Izabela Grobelna, and Mario Longoni, *Legislation Time-Line of American Immigration* (Chicago: Field Museum, Division of Environment, Culture, and Conservation, 2010).

13. This section is based on Chapter 11, "The Segregation and Location of Groups in Cities," of my book *Deciphering the City* (Upper Saddle River, NJ: Prentice Hall, 2005).

14. Robin M. Williams Jr. was a gifted sociologist and prolific writer whose research fostered understanding of some of the most difficult problems of American society, including intergroup tensions, race relations, war and peace, ethnic conflict, and altruism and cooperation. In a series of articles published fifty years ago, he identified core American values, and this research provides the benchmark upon which contemporary research is based.

15. Wayne Baker, *Americans' Evolving Values Surveys* (Ann Arbor: University of Michigan, Institute for Social Research, 2010).

5. THE MELTING POT, MIXED WITH JUST A FEW NEW INGREDIENTS

1. Americans are proud of their ethnic heritages, and we celebrate them in our families and in our popular culture. Americans (85 percent) know their ancestry, because who we are is tied to where we came from, and ancestry.com, genealogy.com, and familysearch.org have profited from uncovering our pasts. Hollywood has tapped into our collective memories with movies about the Irish, like *The Brothers McMullen* (1995), *Far and Away* (1997), and *Mystic River* (2003); the Italians, like *Big Night* (1996), *Mean Streets* (1973), and *Moonstruck* (1981); and the Greeks, like *My Big Fat Greek Wedding* (2002). Not to be overlooked is the current wave of movies on the Latino experience, like *America, The Encounter* (2002), *Against All Odds* (2006), and *American*

Fusion (2005), a film about a couple's romance doomed by the clash between their Chinese and Latino families. Studying popular culture can give additional insight into the assimilation process in American society.

2. Ethnicity, immigration, assimilation, and ethnic experiences are common themes in our literature, cinema, and history. These topics also are important in social science research, and over the past century the original melting pot model has been modified and supplanted with different models as the nature of the assimilation process has changed. Susan Brown and Frank Bean in *New Immigrants, New Models of Assimilation* (Center for Research on Immigration, Population, and Public Policy, University of California–Irvine, 2006) provide a very readable summary of the evolution of these models. I also suggest Mary Waters and Tomás R. Jiménez's "Assessing Immigrant Assimilation: New Empirical and Theoretical Challenges," *Annual Review of Sociology* 31 (2005): 105–25, which examines the assimilation of current immigrants in new southern and midwestern gateways, as well as how sociologists assess their assimilation into American society. Chapter 11, "The Segregation and Location of Groups in Cities," in my *Deciphering the City* provides a broad overview of the process.

3. Migration Policy Institute, "The United States: Social and Demographic Characteristics," MPI Data Hub Web page, accessed April 19, 2012, http://www.migrationinformation.org/datahub.

4. Paul Taylor, preface to "The Rise of Asian Americans," Pew Research Center website, June 19, 2012, http://www.pewsocialtrends.org/files/2012/06/SDT-Rise-of-Asian-Americans.pdf.

5. John R. Logan and Brian J. Stults, "The Persistence of Segregation in the Metropolis: New findings from the 2010 Census," US2010 Project website, March 24, 2011, http://www.s4.brown.edu/us2010/Data/Report/report2.pdf.

6. Daniel T. Lichter, Parisi Momenico, Michael C. Taquino, and Michael Grice, "Residential Segregation in New Hispanic Destinations: Cities, Suburbs, and Rural Communities Compared," *Social Science Research* 39 (2010): 215–30; Mary C. Waters and Tomás R. Jiménez, "Assessing Immigrant Assimilation: New Empirical and Theoretical Challenges," *Annual Review of Sociology* 31 (2010): 105–25.

7. Tomás R. Jiménez, "Immigrants in the United States: How Well Are They Integrating into Society?," Migration Policy Institute website, May 2011, http://www.migrationpolicy.org/pubs/integration-Jimenez.pdf.

8. John R. Logan and Wenquan Zhang, "Global Neighborhoods: New Evidence," US2010 Project website, November 2011, http://www.s4.brown.edu/us2010/Data/Report/globalfinal2.pdf.

9. Aaron Terrazas, "The Economic Integration of Immigrants in the United States: Long- and Short-Term Perspectives," Migration Policy Institute website, July 2011, http://www.migrationpolicy.org/pubs/EconomicIntegration.pdf.

10. Taylor, preface to "The Rise of Asian Americans."

11. Daniel Dockterman, "Country of Origin Profiles," Pew Research Center website, June 27, 2012, http://www.pewhispanic.org/2011/05/26/country-of-origin-profiles.

12. Jiménez, "Immigrants in the United States," 7.

13. Jiménez, "Immigrants in the United States," 5.

14. Jiménez, "Immigrants in the United States," 5.

15. The Pew Research Center reports that language use among Hispanics and

Asians in the United States reflects the patterns of previous immigrant groups. For example, they find that first-generation Hispanics are most proficient in Spanish, with limited English fluency. In the second generation the use of Spanish falls as the use of English rises. By the third generation English use is dominant, although Spanish continues to be used with family and friends. Like native-born Americans, the vast majority (87 percent) of Hispanics believe Hispanic immigrants need to learn English to succeed in the United States. Hispanic adults do not want to turn their backs on their heritage, however. Ninety-five percent believe it is important for future generations of Hispanics to be able to speak Spanish. Language acquisition among Asians is identical. See also Paul Taylor, Mark H. Lopez, Jessica H. Martinez, and Gabriel Velasco, "When Labels Don't Fit: Hispanics and Their Views of Identity," in *Social and Demographic Trends*, ed. Paul Taylor (Washington, D.C.: Pew Research Center, 2012); Taylor, preface to "The Rise of Asian Americans."

16. Pew Research Center, "The Rise of Intermarriage: Rates, Characteristics Vary by Race and Gender," in *Social and Demographic Trends*, ed. Paul Taylor (Washington, D.C.: Pew Research Center, 2012).

17. Mary C. Waters and Tomás R. Jiménez, "Assessing Immigrant Assimilation: New Empirical and Theoretical Challenges," *Annual Review of Sociology* 31 (2010): 105–25.

18. Jiménez, "Immigrants in the United States," 15.

6. THE DREAM ACT

1. Department of Homeland Security, "Secretary Napolitano Announces Deferred Action Process for Young People Who Are Low Enforcement Priorities," Department of Homeland Security website, June 15, 2012, http://www.dhs.gov/ynews/releases/20120612-napolitano-announces-deferred-action-process-for-young-people.shtm.

2. Migration Policy Institute, "As Many as 1.4 Million Unauthorized Immigrant Youth Could Gain Relief from Deportation under Obama Administration Grant of Deferred Action," Migration Policy Institute website, June 15, 2012, http://www.migrationpolicy.org/news/2012_06_15.php.

3. By executive order, President Obama could have granted, on humanitarian grounds, Deferred Enforced Departure (DED) or Temporary Protected Status (TPS). President George W. Bush and other presidents have used these remedies in the past. These statuses carry certain due process protections. Applications can be appealed in immigration court if denied. There is no due process under deferred action; administrative actions are final.

4. There are three major agencies within the Department of Homeland Security: Immigration and Customs Enforcement (ICE), Customs and Border Protection (CBP), and U.S. Citizenship and Immigration Services (USCIS). For more information on the organization and the duties of the department, see Department of Homeland Security website, http://www.dhs.gov/organization.

5. Laura Ferner, e-mail message to author, July 11, 2012.

6. John Morton, "Exercising Prosecutorial Discretion Consistent with the Civil Immigration Enforcement Priorities of the Agency for the Apprehension, Detention, and Removal of Aliens," U.S. Immigration and Customs website, June 17, 2011,

http://www.ice.gov/doclib/secure-communities/pdf/prosecutorial-discretion-memo
.pdf.

7. David Bennion, "Third Time's the Charm? Doubts about Obama's Deferred Action Policy," Citizen Orange website, June 15, 2012, http://www.citizenorange
.com/orange/2012/06/third-times-the-charm-doubts-a.html.

8. "The Dream Act: Creating Opportunities for Immigrant Students and Supporting the U.S. Economy," Immigration Policy Center website, last updated May 18, 2011, http://www.immigrationpolicy.org/just-facts/dream-act.

9. The Department of Homeland Security reports that 308,935 undocumented youth applied for deferred action between August 15 and November 15, 2012, averaging 4,827 cases per day. Only 10,101 requests have been rejected. To date, 53,273 undocumented youth have been approved.

10. *Plyler v. Doe* involved a 1975 law enacted by the Texas state legislature that authorized local school districts to bar undocumented children from enrolling in public schools if they chose to do so. The Tyler Independent School District chose to charge these children tuition. In 1977 defense attorneys filed a class action suit against the school district on behalf of these children, and federal courts ruled in 1977 and 1980 that the state law violated the Equal Protection Clause of the Fourteenth Amendment. After a federal appeals court upheld the district court rulings in 1981, the Tyler school board and school superintendent James Plyler appealed to the Supreme Court. For an excellent overview of the legal background of the DREAM Act and the law behind educating the undocumented, see Vicky J. Salinas, "You Can Be Whatever You Want to Be When You Grow Up, Unless Your Parents Brought You to This Country Illegally: The Struggle to Grant In-State Tuition to Undocumented Immigrant Students," *Houston Law Review* 43 (2006): 847–77.

11. Susana Garcia, "Dream Come True or True Nightmare? The Effect of Creating Educational Opportunity for Undocumented Youth," *Golden Gate University Law Review* 36, no. 2 (2006): 247–68; Youngro Lee, "To Dream or Not to Dream: A Cost-Benefit Analysis of the Development, Relief, and Education for Alien Minors (DREAM) Act," *Cornell Journal of Law and Public Policy* (Fall 2006): 231–61.

12. For an excellent overview of congressional action on the DREAM Act, see Andorra Bruno, "Unauthorized Alien Students: Issues and 'DREAM Act' Legislation," Federation of American Scientists website, June 19, 2012, http://www.fas.org/sgp/crs/misc/RL33863.pdf.

13. Center for American Progress, *Facts of Immigration Today* (Washington, D.C.: Center for American Progress, 2012).

14. Edward Drachman, "Access to Higher Education for Undocumented Students," *Peace Review* 18 (2006): 91–100

15. 8 U.S.C. § 1623(a)

16. In 2005 a bill was introduced in the Arkansas General Assembly that would have allowed in-state tuition for undocumented students who had attended an Arkansas high school for three years. It passed in the House but failed in the Senate. In 2008 the director of the Arkansas Department of Higher Education issued a memorandum, citing two federal laws, requiring incoming students to furnish a valid Social Security number or other proof of citizenship to obtain in-state tuition. Until then, graduates from Arkansas high schools received in-state tuition. Elizabeth Young, a colleague in the law school, provides a compelling brief on the rationale and law

for in-state tuition for undocumented youth. See Elizabeth Young, *Legal Brief on the Issue of Undocumented Students and In-State Tuition at Arkansas Public Universities* (Fayetteville: University of Arkansas, School of Law, 2012).

17. See notes 1 and 2 of the introduction. States that have barred unauthorized immigrant students from in-state tuition benefits include Arizona (Proposition 300, 2006), Colorado (HB 1023, 2006), Georgia (SB 492, 2008), South Carolina (HB 4400, 2008), and Indiana (H 1402, 2011). This information was up to date at the time of publication. In July 2012, I wrote Brenda Bautsch, a researcher at the National Conference of State Legislatures, an organization that tracks state legislation and analyzes legislative trends. She responded, "Wisconsin revoked its law in 2011 with AB 40. As for Oklahoma, there is much confusion over their law. Oklahoma had passed a DREAM Act, but in 2008 their legislature passed HB 1804 which shifted the responsibility for determining its in-state tuition benefits to their Board of Regents. HB 1804 actually did not end the in-state tuition benefit. It changed the statutory language from the 'Board of Regents SHALL' offer an in-state tuition benefit for undocumented students to the 'Board of Regents MAY.' So it's left up to the board to decide." Brenda Bautsch, e-mail message to author, July 20, 2012. I wrote the Oklahoma State Board of Regents for Higher Education and received an e-mail from their general counsel. The criteria he cited show that the regent's interpretation of Oklahoma's law is the same as the other DREAM Act states. Ann Morse and Kerry Bimbach, *In-State Tuition and Unauthorized Immigrant Students* (Washington, D.C.: National Conference of State Legislatures, 2011); National Immigration Law Center, *Basic Facts about In-State Tuition for Undocumented Immigrant Students* (Washington, D.C.: National Immigration Law Center, 2012).

18. In December 2010 the Migration Policy Institute updated their analysis and lowered the potential beneficiaries of the DREAM Act to 1,974,000 based on the pending legislation in Congress. These and subsequent bills have not passed, and I have decided to use the estimates in the original study. For a copy of the study, see Migration Policy Institute, "MPI Updates National and State-Level Estimates of Potential DREAM Act Beneficiaries," Migration Policy Institute website, December 2010, http://www.migrationpolicy.org/pubs/DREAM-Update-December2010.pdf.

19. Congressional Budget Office, *S. 3992: Development, Relief, and Education for Alien Minors Act of 2010* (Washington, D.C.: U.S. Congress, Congressional Budget Office, 2010).

20. Hinojosa-Ojeda and Takash, *No Dreamers Left Behind*.

21. Roberto G. Gonzales, *Young Lives on Hold: The College Dreams of Undocumented Students* (Reston, VA: College Board Advocacy and Policy Center, 2009), 23.

22. Robert B. Stromberg, *Extending In-State Tuition to Undocumented Immigrants: Policy Analysis of North Carolina House Bill 1183* (Raleigh, NC: North Carolina State University, School of Public and International Affairs, Policy Analysis Project, 2006).

23. Memorandum from the Office of the Chancellor to the Honorable Davy Carter, September 3, 2010.

24. Kimberly Mehlman-Orozco, *The Effects of In-State Tuition for Non-citizens: A Systematic Review of the Evidence* (Providence, RI: Roger Williams University, Latino Policy Institute, 2011).

25. Gonzales, "Wasted Talent and Broken Dreams," 12.

26. Raúl Hinojosa-Ojeda, *Raising the Floor for American Workers: The Economic*

Benefits of Comprehensive Immigration Reform (Washington: Center for American Progress Immigration Policy Center, 2010).

27. Aaron Terrazas, *Migration and Development: Policy Perspectives from the United State* (Washington, D.C.: Migration Policy Institute, 2011).

28. Georges Vernez, Richard A. Krop, and C. Peter Rydell, *Closing the Education Gap: Benefits and Costs* (Santa Monica, CA: RAND Education, 1999).

29. Carol Morello and Luz Lazo, "Baltimore Puts Out Welcome Mat for Immigrants, Hoping to Stop Population Decline," *Washington Post,* July 24, 2012.

30. Lee, "To Dream or Not to Dream."

31. William H. Frey, "Baby Boomers Had Better Embrace Change," *Washington Post,* June 8, 2012.

7. MEET TWO DREAMERS

1. Richard Fry and Mark Hugo Lopez, "Hispanic Student Enrollments Reach New Highs in 2011," Pew Research Center website, August 20, 2012, http://www.pewhispanic.org/2012/08/20/hispanic-student-enrollments-reach-new-highs-in-2011.

2. A video recording of the program is available at http://chancellor.uark.edu/17056.php.

8. NEXT STEPS

1. Miriam Jordan, "Tech Titans Fund Undocumented Students," *Wall Street Journal,* March 6, 2012.

2. Jeffrey M. Jones, "Americans More Positive about Immigration: Sixty-six Percent Say It Is a Good Thing for U.S., Highest since 2006," June 16, 2012, http://www.gallup.com/poll/155210/Americans-Positive-Immigration.aspx.

3. Stephanie Condon, "Most Likely Voters Approve of Obama's New Immigration Policy, Poll Shows," CBS News website, June 19, 2012, http://www.cbsnews.com/8301-503544_162-57455918-503544/most-likely-voters-approve-of-obamas-new-immigration-policy-poll-shows.

4. There is some question as to whether Rosa Parks's refusal to move to the back of the bus was a spontaneous or a planned protest. My colleague Calvin White, professor of history and director of the University of Arkansas's African and African American Studies Program, believes it was a planned protest. Rosa Parks had received training in nonviolence by organizers of the NAACP in the months prior to December 1. If not planned, she was prepared for the events that followed. Paulina Gonzalez, an activist and historian of the DREAM movement, agrees with White's analysis.

5. Sociology emerged in the wake of the French Revolution two centuries ago, and social movements have been a research focus throughout the discipline's history. Not all social movements succeed, but those that do tend to go through the same three stages: preliminary, coalescence, and institutionalization. There are competing sociological theories, but I use Neil Smelser's value-added theory and Mayer Zald's resource mobilization theory. See Diana Kendall, *Sociology in Our Times* (Belmont, CA: Wadsworth, 2012), Chapter 15, for a brief overview of the these theories. I also

draw upon Charles Duhigg, "Saddleback Church and the Montgomery Bus Boycott: How Movements Happen," in his *The Power of Habit: Why We Do What We Do in Life and Business* (New York: Random House, 2012). Duhigg employs social network analysis, which I find, in my lectures and talks, more appealing to a general audience.

6. Paulina Gonzalez was arrested two years ago in a nonviolent civil disobedience action protesting Arizona's anti-immigrant bill SB 1070. She has firsthand knowledge of the movement and its organization, strategy, and efforts leading to the Department of Homeland Security's new policy of deferred action. In July 2012 she published a two-part series on these efforts. Paulina Gonzalez, "The Strategy and Organizing Behind the Successful DREAM Act Movement: Undocumented Youth Have Shown That Ordinary People Build Extraordinary People Power, Even in the United States," *Narco News Bulletin* website, July 10, 2012, http://www.narconews .com/Issue67/article4607.html#.UBgqydDXleA.email. Ms. Gonzalez has graciously permitted me to use her account in this book.

7. Gonzalez, "The Strategy and Organizing Behind the Successful DREAM Act Movement."

8. Gonzalez, "The Strategy and Organizing Behind the Successful DREAM Act Movement."

INDEX

Obama Administration, 10, 25, 40, 44,
    81–85, 120, 126, 125–127
    announcement of Deferred
        Action, 81

Parks, Rosa, 121–123
Personal Responsibility and Work
    Opportunity Reconciliation Act
    (PRWORA), 17
    impact on undocumented youth, 86
push-pull model, 30–35, 53
    barriers, 31
    pull factors, 31
    push factors, 31
    serial migration, 34
    social networks, 31
    See also immigration
Plyler v. Doe, 8, 9, 17–20, 26–27, 74,
    85–87
    Equal Protection Clause, 14th
        Amendment, 18

residential integration, 67–71
    ethnic neighborhoods, 67–69
    generational effect, 69–70
    residential patterns, 70–71
    role of enclaves, 67–68
    spatial diffusion, 69–70
Riverside, New Jersey's anti-
    immigration ordinance, 43
    See anti-immigration laws
    city ordinance, 43
    economic impact, 43
    unintended consequences, 43

self-deportation, 20–24, 106, 113
    language barriers, 22

legal limbo, 24
mixed-status families, 21
reality of, 20–21
school policies, 22
social networks, 23
U.S. Immigration process, 20
Selig Center for Economic Growth,
    44–45
social networks, 5, 6, 23, 30–31, 33, 106
socioeconomic integration, 71–73
    characteristics of Asian and
        Hispanic labor forces, 72–73
    evidence of integration, 73
    implications for DREAM Act, 73

2012 presidential election, 10, 14, 16, 120
    immigrant vote, 120
    political landscape, 120
    Republicans for Immigration
        Reform PAC, 14

undocumented youth, 26–27
    blameless, 26
    life-time income loss, 26
    out-of-state tuition costs, 26–27
    See also Justice William Brennan;
        Plyler v. Doe

United We Dream Network, 10, 21, 99,
    108, 123–128
    See Dream Act Movement
    goals, 123–124
    legal opinion, 126
    rule of small victories, 125–126
    strategies, 124
    success, 127